LAYMAN'S GUIDE TO CRIMINAL LAW AND ANTI-CORRUPTION LAW

Spectrum Law Series

LAYMAN'S GUIDE TO CRIMINAL LAW AND ANTI-CORRUPTION LAW

A. A. Kolajo

Spectrum Books Limited
Ibadan
Abuja • Benin City • Lagos • Owerri

Spectrum titles can be purchased on line at
www.spectrumbooksonline.com

Published by
Spectrum Books Limited
Spectrum House
Ring Road
PMB 5612
Ibadan, Nigeria

in association with
Safari Books (Export) Limited
1st Floor
17 Bond Street
St. Helier
Jersey JE2 3NP
Channel Islands
United Kingdom

Europe and USA Distributor
African Books Collective Ltd.
The Jam Factory
27 Park End Street
Oxford OX1, 1HU, UK

First published, 2002

ISBN: 978-029-338-8

Printed by Kenbim Press Ltd.

Contents

Foreword

The title of this book: *Layman's Guide to Criminal Law and Anti-Corruption Law* has clearly shown the intention of the author. That intention is to educate the layman on criminal law as contained in the Criminal Code and Corrupt Practices and other Related Offences Act, 2000 otherwise known as the Anti-Corruption Law.

The Hon. Justice A. A. Kolajo, who is the author of this book, seems to have a burning desire to educate the layman on the law. I say this because this is his second book on law for the layman. The first title *Laws for the Layman* deals exclusively with Civil Law. This one deals with Criminal Law.

In the advanced countries of Europe and the Americas opportunities abound for the layman to have knowledge of the law. Here in Nigeria such opportunities are limited if not totally lacking. It is in order to make amends for this lack that the Hon. Justice Kolajo had written this book.

The book is written in such a way that any layman, who has a good grounding in the English Language, will understand it.

The book does not of course cover the whole field of Criminal Law but it treats a lot of the offences under the Criminal Code and all the offences under The Corrupt Practices and other Related Offences, Act 2000.

I strongly recommend this book to all laymen who wish to acquire a knowledge of the Criminal Law. Lawyers and Judges will also read the book with profit.

Hon. Justice E. Kolawole
Retired Judge of Osun State,
Bodija Estate, Ibadan
April, 2001

Preface

This book is primarily for the layman, that is, one who is not learned in the law. This book deals with criminal matters. Everybody should know a little bit about the Criminal Law so that he may not run foul of the law that governs him. Ignorance of the law is generally not a valid defence in a criminal case.

Some legal terms are defined in chapter one of the book. Some technical words or phrases are explained in simple language. I do not number the sections of the Criminal Code because they are not uniform all over the country. Sections in the Codes of the Federal and States enactments differ.

Some States omit some of the sections while others put in more than the sections in the Federal Criminal Code Act. Some States have additional sections or sub-sections. The sections differ from State to State and some States even differ from the Federal Criminal Code Act.

To number the sections will therefore be misleading. Punishment in the Codes is not uniform. But I cite the sections of the Anti-Corruption Law because only the Federal Government has so far enacted such law. Some decided cases are referred to but their citations are deliberately omitted to make the book easy to read. Though this book is essentially for laymen (a term which includes lay women), law students, lawyers and judges can read it with profit. Learned brothers and acquaintances who read my *Laws for Layman* call on me for a write-up on Criminal Law. This is to meet their yearnings.

Hon. Justice A. A. Kolajo
Plot 6 Oyewusi Lay-out,
Old Ife Road, Agodi,
Ibadan.
21 April, 2001

Acknowledgement

I thank God Almighty who made the writing of this book a reality. I thank Him for giving me the inspiration, wisdom and good health to write the book.

I acknowledge the assistance given by Hon. Justice Ekundayo Kolawole in painstakingly reading through the draft, making necessary corrections and offering useful suggestions thereon. I also thank His Lordship for his elucidating Foreword to the book.

I read through a number of books in the course of writing this book; prominent among them are Brett and Mclean's *The Criminal Law and Procedure of the Six Southern States of Nigeria* and Okonkwo and Naish: *Criminal Law in Nigeria*. I thank the learned authors of these books.

In the home front, I thank my wife and children who gave me the peace of mind which rendered the job an easy one. I also thank my typists for a job well done.

Hon. Justice A. A. Kolajo
Plot 6 Oyewusi Lay-out,
Old Ife Road, Agodi,
Ibadan.
21 April, 2001

CHAPTER 1

General Principles

Definition of Crime
A crime is an act or omission which renders the person doing the act or making the omission liable to punishment under the Criminal Code or under any law or statute. It is a breach of public law.

An act is regarded as a crime if it is an injury or wrong to the community, whereas a tort is a wrong to an individual.

Crime may simply be defined as an offence for which one may be punished by law.

Division of Offences
Offences are of three kinds, namely **felonies, misdemeanours** and **simple offences.**

Felony
A felony is any offence which is declared by law to be a felony, or is punishable, without proof of previous conviction, with death or with imprisonment for three years or more.

Misdemeanour
A misdemeanour is an offence which is declared by law to be a misdemeanour, or is punishable by imprisonment for not less than six months, but less than three years.

Simple Offences
All offences, other than felonies and misdemeanours, are simple offences.

1

Principal Offenders

When an offence is committed, each of the following persons is deemed to have taken part in committing the offence and to be guilty of the offence, and may be charged with actually committing it, that is:

(a) every person who actually does the act or makes the commission which constitutes the offence;

(b) every person who does or omits to do any act for the purpose of enabling or aiding another person to commit the offence;

(c) every person who aids another person in committing the offence;

(d) any person who counsels or procures any other person to commit the offence.

When two or more persons form a common intention to prosecute an unlawful purpose in conjunction with one another, and in the prosecution of such purpose an offence is committed of such a nature that its commission was a probable consequence of the prosecution of such purpose, each of them is deemed to have committed the offence.

A person who receives or assists another who is, to his knowledge guilty of an offence, in order to enable him to escape punishment, is said to become an accessory after the fact to the offence.

A wife does not become an accessory after the fact to an offence of which the husband is guilty by receiving or assisting him to escape punishment.

Under (a) above, the man who sticks the knife in is the man who does the act of murder.

The man who loans an instrument, e.g., a rope, a matchet, a car, to any intending criminal for the commission of an offence comes under (b) above.

Under (c) the assistance in commission of an offence must fall short of the actual commission of the unlawful act itself, otherwise (a) above would apply.

If the aid is not given either prior to, or at the time of, the commission of the offence but is given afterwards, then, the accused cannot be a principal but only an accessory after the fact.

Kinds of Punishment

Subject to the provision of any other written law, the punishment which may be inflicted under this Code are: death, imprisonment, whipping, fine and forfeiture. The court has a general power to inflict a fine instead of imprisonment even where the law creating the offence only refers to imprisonment.

Criminal Responsibility

As a general rule, the law does not punish omission; majority of crimes can be committed only by the doing of something. For instance, it is no offence for a person to stand by and watch a baby crawl into a deep well, when it is within his reach to save the baby's life. A person who stands by as a cigarette butt sets fire to another person's house commits no offence even though he could easily have put out the cigarette's fire by merely stamping his feet on it. The person who fails to save a baby from crawling into a deep well or to quench cigarette fire may be morally or religiously reprehensible, but he has not committed any offence in law. He cannot be punished for his moral or religious laxity.

Criminal responsibility means liability for an offence. The conditions or circumstances below may affect criminal responsibility.

Ignorance of the Law

This does not afford any excuse for any act or omission which would otherwise constitute an offence, unless knowledge of the law by the offender is expressly declared to be an element of the offence.

Bona Fide Claim of Right

A person is not criminally responsible as for an offence relating to property, for an act done or omitted to be done by him with respect to any property in the exercise of an honest claim of right and without intention to defraud. Property includes everything animate or inanimate capable of being the subject of ownership. Honest claim of right affords a good defence on a charge of wilful or unlawful damage to property.

A person who set up an unauthorised court could have no honest claim of right to enforce payment of an alleged debt by beating and imprisonment of the debtor without allowing him to state his case.

This defence was held to afford a justification on a charge of wilful or unlawful damage to property.

A man taking possession of property must believe not merely that it is his own but that he is entitled to immediate possession of it.

Intention: Motive

A person is not criminally responsible for an act or omission which occurs by accident. Unless otherwise expressly declared, the motive by which a person is induced to do or omit to do an act, or to form an intention, is immaterial as regards criminal responsibility. For example, a man who steals a loaf of bread to feed his children commits the offence of stealing although his motive is to save children from starvation because he has intent permanently to deprive the owner of the property. People who, out of pity, kill a suffering relation at his request are guilty of murder. A person who discharges a firearm unintentionally and without attendant criminal malice or negligence will not be liable both for the firing and for its consequences. Where a person discharges a firearm intentionally, and without either criminal malice or negligence on his part and the bullet strikes someone else and injure him, the injury to the other person will be treated as having occurred by accident. The position is different if the shooting is a deliberate act. In the latter case a charge of discharging a firearm in a township would lie, but not one of homicide or unlawful wounding.

Accident

A person is not criminally responsible for an event which occurs by accident. An accused is not held liable for any accidental event simply because it results from an unlawful act committed by him. An accused only has to make a defence if the prosecution has proved that the event was intended and not an accident.

In a decided case, the deceased gripped the appellant's gun. In an attempt to recover it from him the appellant accidentally touched the trigger and the gun went off and killed the deceased. The event was held to be an accident and the appellant was not guilty of killing the deceased. In another case, two school boys A and B were pushing each other near a river. A third boy warned them that they were playing a dangerous game. Following a push by A, B slipped, fell into the river and was drowned, it was held that B's death was not an accidental event because a reasonable person would have appreciated the danger of pushing another near a river in the circumstances.

Insanity

Every person is presumed to be of sound mind, and to have been of sound mind at any time in question, until the contrary is proved. A person is not criminally responsible for an act or omission if at the time of doing the act or making the omission he is in such a state of mental disease or natural mental infirmity as to deprive him of capacity to understand what he is doing or of capacity to control his actions or of capacity to know that he ought not to do the act or make the omission. A person whose mind, at the time of his doing or omitting to do an act, is affected by delusion on some specific matter or matters, but who is not otherwise entitled to the benefit of the foregoing provisions of this section, is criminally responsible for the act or omission to the same extent as if the real state of things had been such as he was induced by the delusions to believe to exist.

The defect in mental power must not be produced by the accused's own default. The relevant time of the insanity is the time of the commission of the unlawful act. The fact that an accused is sane at his trial is irrelevant. Nor does insanity at the time of trial prove insanity at the time of the act.

Insanity is a defence because it prevents the exercise of the will. To establish insanity and to overcome the presumption that everyman is sane and accountable for his actions, the defence must prove, first that the accused was at the relevant time suffering either from mental disease or from natural infirmity, and secondly that the mental disease or natural infirmity was such that at the relevant time, the accused was as a result deprived of capacity:

(a) to understand what he was doing; or

(b) to control his actions; or

(c) to know that he ought not to do the act or make the omission.

Mistake of Fact
A person who does or omits to do an act under an honest and reasonable, but mistaken belief in the existence of any state of things is not criminally responsible for the act or omission to any greater extent than if the real state of things has been such as he believed to exist. The belief must be reasonable. A belief in witchcraft has been held not reasonable. Also a belief held in reckless disregard of assurance which a man ought in the circumstances to be able to rely on is not an honest and reasonable belief.

The mistake must be a mistaken belief in the existence of any state of things. Mistake of law is irrelevant because ignorance of the law does not afford any excuse for any act or omission which would otherwise constitute an offence, unless knowledge of the law by the offender is expressly declared to be an element of the offence. In a decided case, one of the accused said at his trial that he did not know that it was contrary to law to pay a bribe in order to induce the other accused to appoint him as village headman and tax collector. The trial judge accepted this story and acquitted him. On appeal it was held that on a charge involving doing some act corruptly, ignorance of the law is not a defence to a person who had an intent of a kind which the law regards as corrupt.

A mistake must be both honest and reasonable. In a decided case, the accused believed that the miscarriage and mortal illness of his wife was due to the witchcraft of an old woman and he killed the latter with a bow. The accused's belief was bona fide and a belief in witchcraft was prevalent in the community in which he lived. The accused was convicted of murder, holding the mistake to be unreasonable. In some cases the definition of an offence may exclude the defence of mistake.

Extraordinary Emergencies

Subject to the express provision of the Criminal Code relating to acts done upon compulsion or provocation or in self-defence, a person is not criminally responsible for an act done or omission made under such circumstances of sudden or extraordinary emergency that an ordinary person possessing ordinary powers of self-control could not reasonably be expected to act otherwise.

Compulsion arising from hunger or from immediate danger to a person's life or property will not excuse the commission of a crime, but where the emergency is either sudden or extraordinary, it appears that either of these causes is capable of affording a defence. The courts would be more ready to hold that this provision applied where there was immediate danger to life than in other circumstances.

Intoxication

Save as provided hereunder intoxication shall not constitute a defence to any criminal charge. Intoxication shall be a defence to a criminal charge if by reason thereof the person charged at the time of the act or omission complained of did not know that such act or omission was wrong or did not know what he was doing and:

(a) the state of intoxication was caused without his consent by the malicious or negligent act of another person; or

(b) the person charged was by reason of intoxication temporarily insane or otherwise at the time of such act or omission.

Intoxication shall be taken into account for the purpose of determining whether the person charged had formed any intention, specific or otherwise, in the absence of which he would not be guilty of the offence. Intoxication includes a state produced by narcotics or drugs. The burden of proof of intoxication as a defence is on the person charged.

Immature Age
A person under the age of seven years is not criminally responsible for any act done or omission. A person under the age of twelve years is not criminally responsible for an act of omission, unless it is proved that at the time of doing the act or making the omission he had capacity to know that he ought not to do the act ort make the omission.

A male person under the age of twelve years is presumed to be incapable of having carnal knowledge. This is merely a presumption which is rebuttable.

Judicial Officers
Except as expressly provided by the Criminal Code, a judicial officer is not criminally responsible for anything done or omitted to be done by him in the exercise of his judicial function, although the act done is in excess of his judicial authority or although he is bound to do the act omitted to be done.

Justification and Excuse
A person is not criminally responsible for an act or omission if he does or omits to do the act under any of the following circumstances:

(i) in execution of the law. Thus the hangman who carried out a judicial execution is protected from prosecution for doing his lawful duty;

(ii) in obedience to the order of a competent authority which he is bound to obey, unless the order is manifestly unlawful. This gives a limited protection in all circumstances to members of the Military and Police Forces.

(iii) where the act is reasonably necessary in order to resist actual and unlawful violence threatened to him, or to another person;

(iv) where he does or omits to do the act in order to save himself from immediate death or grievous harm. Like in above, this provision would not cover acts done to avoid danger arising from natural causes, e.g. from a mad dog or a fire.

Compulsion of Husband

A married woman is not free from criminal responsibility for doing or omitting to do an act merely because the act or omission takes place in the presence of her husband. But the wife of a Christian marriage is not criminally responsible for doing or omitting to do an act which she is actually compelled by her husband to do or omit to do.

The section affords a defence to the wife personally, but does not alter the nature of her act or omission, and the husband may be convicted in respect of it as a principal offender. A husband and wife of a Christian marriage are not criminally responsible for a conspiracy between themselves alone.

Liability of Husband and Wife for Offences Committed by Either with Respect to the Other's Property

When a husband and wife of a Christian marriage are living together, neither of them incurs any criminal responsibility for doing or omitting to do any act with respect to the property of the other, except in the case of an act or omission of which an intention to injure or defraud some other person is an element and except in the case of an act done by either of them leaving or deserting, or when about to leave or desert the other.

Subject to the foregoing provisions, a husband and wife are each of them criminally responsible for an act, by him or her, with respect to the separate property of the other, which would be an offence if they were not husband and wife, and to the same extent as if they were not husband and wife. But in the case of a Christian marriage neither of them can institute criminal proceedings against the other while they are living together.

Neither the husband nor the wife can incur criminal responsibility for doing any acts in respect of each other's property. Thus, a husband cannot be charged with wilfully setting fire to his wife's house. This rule applies only to offences against property. A husband can be guilty of assaulting his wife, however minor the assault. A husband cannot be guilty of any offence involving "unlawful carnal knowledge in respect of his wife but he can be guilty of indecent assault on her" where the marriage was conducted under native law and custom.

Offences by Partners and Members of Companies with Respect to Partnership or Corporate Property

A person who, being a member of a partnership, corporation, or joint stock company, does or omits to do any act with respect to the property of the partnership, corporation, or company, which would constitute an offence is criminally responsible to the same extent as if he were not such member.

Automatism

A defence of automatism may arise when a man acts in a state of unconsciousness. Automatism is different from insanity. In insanity the onus of proof is on the defence, while in automatism the general onus on the prosecution is undisturbed. If the accused can reasonably prevent the conduct which he claims as automatic then he has no defence.

A driver who allows himself to fall asleep at the wheel of a motor car cannot claim automatism as a defence because when he realised he was falling asleep he should have stopped his car. But a man should not be liable for resulting injuries if he lost control of the car he was driving as a result of being struck by a stone, overcome by sudden illness, or attacked by a swarm of bees. Spasm, reflex action, convulsion and sleep walking may be genuine cases of automatism.

In a decided case, the accused claimed that his erratic driving was due to an attack of epilepsy and a medical witness for the prosecution supported this. The prosecution did not produce any evidence to disprove the evidence of the medical witness. Thus the court acquitted the accused.

CHAPTER 2

Preliminary Offences

Attempt

When a person, intending to commit an offence, begins to put his intention into execution by means adapted to its fulfilment, and manifests his intention by some overt act, but does not fulfil his intention to such an extent as to commit the offence, he is said to attempt to commit the offence. It is immaterial, except so far as regards punishment, whether the offender does all that is necessary on his part for completing the commission of the offence, or whether the complete fulfilment of his intention is prevented by circumstances independent of his will, or whether he desists of his own motion from further prosecution of his intention.

It is immaterial that by reason of circumstances not known to the offender it is impossible in fact to commit the offence. The same facts may constitute one offence and an attempt to commit another offence.

In a decided case, an accused person offered to print currency notes in return for money and, after a trap had been set for him, he was arrested before he could set his printing outfit in operation. It was held that he could not be convicted of attempting to obtain by false pretences and that at most there was a preparation for the commission of a crime.

In a case of attempt to commit a crime, the prosecution must prove that the steps taken by the accused must have reached the point where they indicate beyond reasonable doubt what was the end of which they were directed. In other words, the prosecution must prove something more than mere preparation and must show that the accused took an actual step in the commission of the crime.

But a man may be convicted of an attempt although based on the actual facts, the crime attempted was physically incapable of completion. For example, A is guilty of attempted murder if he fires a pistol at B with the intention of killing B who, unknown to A, had died of heart failure a short time before. Similarly an accused can be convicted of trying to "pick" an empty pocket.

In one case, a jeweller hid his jewellery, tied himself up and pretended that his shop was burgled. His object was to collect the insurance money, but he was arrested before he had made any claim. It was held that he was not guilty of attempt. If he had made a claim of the money from the insurance company or had communicated to the company the facts of the pretended burglary upon which a claim was to be subsequently based, he clearly could have been convicted.

In another case a Native Court clerk accepted a cow with the promise that he would use his influence on the court to obtain the donor's acquittal on a criminal charge. It was held that the mere promise does not constitute the attempt. The receipt of a sum of money for the purpose of making counterfeit coins was held not sufficient to constitute an attempt to make or begin to make any counterfeit gold or silver coin. But an accused who was a handcuffed prisoner was guilty of attempting to escape when he broke the handcuff.

A salesman was entitled to commission on cars sold through him. The procedure for payment was that he prepared a voucher for his entitlement and after approval by the Sales Manager and the Chief Accountant, it was presented to the Cashier for payment. He forged the signature of the Sales Manager on a voucher prepared by himself and presented it to the Chief Accountant for payment. The latter was dissatisfied and wanted to see the Sales Manager personally, whereupon the accused seized the voucher and ran away destroying part of it before he was apprehended. He was convicted of attempting to steal the amount on the voucher.

Conspiracy

Conspiracy is an agreement of two or more persons to do an act which it is an offence to agree to do. It may also be described as an agreement of two or more persons to do an unlawful act or to do a lawful act by unlawful means.

A trial court may infer compliance from the fact of doing things towards a common end. While a mere future intention is not punishable as a conspiracy even if two or more persons share it, the offence of conspiracy is complete as soon as two or more agree to carry the intention into effect.

There can be no conspiracy if there is no genuine agreement, as where one party pretends to enter into an agreement in order to build up incriminating evidence against the other.

Conspiracy to commit a felony is itself a felony and the offender is liable, if no other punishment is provided, to imprisonment for seven years.

Conspiracy to commit a misdemeanour is also a felony punishable with seven years imprisonment. The offender can be arrested without a warrant.

Conspiracies other than those earlier mentioned are misdemeanours and the offender is liable to imprisonment for two years. If an accused is found not guilty of the substantive offence, he cannot be guilty of conspiracy.

CHAPTER 3

Offences Against Public Order

Treason

Any person who levies war against the State, in order to intimidate or overawe the President or the Governor of the State, is guilty of treason, and is liable to the punishment of death. Any person conspiring with any person, either within or without Nigeria, to levy war against the State with intent to cause such levying of war as would be treason if committed by a citizen of Nigeria is guilty and is liable to the punishment of death.

Treason may be committed against Nigeria by any person, whether or not he is a citizen of Nigeria, as long as some act connected with the treason is done or has effect in a place which makes the Code apply to him. Treason is essentially an offence against the duty of allegiance and it is not the practice to charge foreigners with treason by virtue of acts done in a foreign country, or by members of the Armed Forces, unless the offence was committed in breach of such duty.

A person conspiring with any person either within or outside Nigeria to levy war against the State is guilty of treason. Any person who instigates any foreigner to invade Nigeria with an armed force is guilty of treason and is liable to the punishment of death. To instigate war means to attempt to procure war. It need not be shown that an invasion took place.

There is no difference between intimidating and overawing the State and doing the same to the Head of State for as the Head of State, he is the embodiment of the State; to intimidate him is the same as intimidating the State.

Concealment of Treason

Any person who:

(i)   becomes an accessory after the fact to treason; or

(ii) knowing that any person intends to commit treason, does not give information thereof with all reasonable despatch to the President or the Governor of the State or a Peace Officer, or use other reasonable endeavours to prevent the commission of the offence;

is guilty of a felony, and is liable to imprisonment for life.

Treasonable Felonies

Any person who forms an intention to effect any of the following purposes, that is:

(a) to remove during his term of office otherwise than by constitutional means the President of the Federal Republic as Head of State of the Federation and Commander-in-Chief of the Armed Forces; or

(b) to levy war against Nigeria in order by force of constraint to compel the President to change his measures or counsels, or in order to put any force or constraint upon, or in order to intimidate or overawe any House of Parliament or any other Legislature or legislative authority; or

(c) to instigate any foreigner to make any armed invasion of Nigeria or any of the territories thereof and manifest such intention by an overt act;

is guilty of a felony and is liable to imprisonment for life.

Intimidating or overawing does not necessarily involve putting the Head of State into fear for his personal safety. It involves creating a situation where the government feels compelled to choose between yielding to force or exposing its members or the public to very serious danger.

Inciting to Mutiny

Any person who advisedly attempts to effect any of the following purposes, that is:

(a) to seduce any person serving in any of the Armed Forces of Nigeria or any member of the Police Force from his duty and allegiance to the President; or

(b) to incite any such persons to commit any act of mutiny or any traitorous or mutinous act; or

(c) to incite any such persons to make or endeavour to make a mutinous assembly;

  is guilty of a felony, and is liable to imprisonment for life.

"Advisedly" in this provision means "deliberately" or "intentionally."

Sedition

Any person who:

(a) does or attempts to do, or makes any preparation to do or conspires with any person to do, any act with seditious intention;

(b) utters any seditious words;

(c) prints, publishes, sells, offers for sale, distributes or reproduces any seditious publications;

(d) imports any seditious publication, unless he has no reason to believe that it is seditious;

  shall be guilty of an offence and liable on conviction for a first offence to imprisonment for two years or to a fine of two hundred naira or to both such imprisonment for three years, and any seditious publication shall be forfeited to the State.

Any person who without lawful excuse has in his possession any seditious publication shall be guilty of an offence and liable on conviction, for a first offence to imprisonment for one year or to a fine of one hundred naira or to both such imprisonment and fine, and for a subsequent offence to imprisonment for two years, and such publication shall be forfeited to the State.

A seditious intention is an intention:

(a) to bring into hatred or contempt or to excite disaffection against the person of the President, or the Governor of a State, or the Government of the Federation, or of any State thereof, as by law established or against the administration of justice in Nigeria; or

(b) to excite the citizens or other inhabitants of Nigeria to attempt to procure the alteration, otherwise than by lawful means, of any other matter in Nigeria as by law established, or

(c) to raise discontent or disaffection among the citizens or other inhabitants of Nigeria; or

(d) to promote feelings of ill-will and hostility between different classes of the population of Nigeria.

A person has a right to discuss any grievance or criticise, canvass and censure the acts of government and their public policy. He may even do this with a view to effecting a change in the party in power or to call attention to the weakness of a government, so long as he keeps within the limits of fair criticism. It is clearly legitimate and constitutional by means of fair argument to criticise the government of the day. What is not permitted is to criticise the government in a malignant manner for such attacks, by their nature tend to affect the public peace.

He who writes an article with a seditious intention cannot by including in the article criticism which is legitimate be excused from a charge of writing a seditious article. At times a seditious article contains parts which are not seditious. These parts do not excuse the article from being seditious.

Provided that the seditious intention is clear, a publication does not cease to be seditious merely because it does not tend to incite people to violence. Violence is not a necessary ingredient of the offence of sedition. What the offence is concerned with is "attacks which by their nature tend to affect public peace".

Truth cannot be a defence to a charge of sedition, but it may in certain circumstances be a relevant consideration for the purpose of ascertaining the real intention of the person charged.

CHAPTER 4

Breaches of the Peace

Unlawful Societies

Any person who:

(a) is a member of an unlawful society; or

(b) knowingly allows a meeting of unlawful society, or of members of an unlawful society, to be held in any house, building, or place belonging to, or occupied by him or over which he has control;

is guilty of a felony and is liable to imprisonment for three years.

A society includes any combination of ten or more persons whether the society be known by any name or not.

(i) A society is an unlawful society if formed for any of the following purposes:

    (a) levying war or encouraging or assisting any person to levy war on the Government or the inhabitants of any part of Nigeria; or

    (b) killing or injuring of any person; or

    (c) destroying or injuring or encouraging the destruction or injuring of any property; or

    (d) subverting or promoting the subversion of the Government or its officials; or

    (e) committing or inciting to acts of violence or intimidation; or

    (f) interfering with or resisting, or encouraging interference with or resistance to the administration of the law; or

(g)   disturbing or encouraging the disturbance of peace and order in any part of Nigeria; or

(ii) A society is an unlawful society if declared by an order of the Minister to be a society dangerous to the good governance of Nigeria or of any part thereof.

The prevalent secret cults in our institutions of learning and other places are no doubt unlawful societies under the Criminal Code. But apart from the Criminal Code there are now stringent laws against membership of secret societies and cults. Violation of the laws attract severe punishment.

Our Constitution which is the supreme law of our land frowns at secret societies and cults. Subsection (4) of section 38 of the 1999 Constitution of the Federal Republic of Nigeria stipulates that nothing in the section shall entitle any person to form, take part in the activity or be a member of a secret society.

Managing an Unlawful Society
Any person who manages or assists in the management of an unlawful society is guilty of a felony and is liable to imprisonment for seven years.

Any person who:

(a)   is a member of an unlawful society; or

(b)   knowingly allows a meeting of an unlawful society, or of members of an unlawful society, to be held in any house, buildings, or place belonging to or occupied by him or over which he has control;
is guilty of a felony and is liable to imprisonment for three years.

Unlawful Assemblies
When three or more persons, with intent to carry out some common purpose, assemble in such a manner or being assembled, conduct themselves in such a manner as to cause persons in the neighbourhood to fear on reasonable grounds that

the persons so assembled will tumultuously disturb the peace or will by such assembly needlessly and without any reasonable occasion provoke other persons tumultuously to disturb the peace, they are an unlawful assembly.

It is immaterial that the original assembling was lawful if, being assembled they conduct themselves with a common purpose in such a manner as aforesaid.

An assembly of three or more persons who assembled for the purpose of protecting any house against persons threatening to break and enter the house in order to commit a felony or misdemeanour therein is not an unlawful assembly.

When an unlawful assembly has begun to act in so tumultuous a manner as to disturb the peace, the assembly is called a riot, and the persons assembled are said to be riotously assembled.

Any person who takes part in an unlawful assembly is guilty of a misdemeanour, and is liable to imprisonment for one year. But any person who takes part in a riot is guilty of felony, and is liable to imprisonment for three years.

An unlawful assembly or riot, need not occur in a public place. If a casual crowd starts a fight they do not thereby become an unlawful assembly for the reason that when they gathered they did not do so with intent to carry out any common purpose. Such an assembly cannot become an unlawful assembly unless it breaks up into groups with intent to carry out some common purpose.

Where a crowd of about 500 people congregated on a public highway, brandishing lethal weapons, singing songs, obstructing the highway with palm leaves and cut a tree across the road it was held that they constituted an unlawful assembly. If a casual crowd starts a fight, it is merely a sudden affray: four or five or ten of them may attack some others: that does not make them an unlawful assembly or a riotous assembly for the reason that when they gathered they did not do so with the intent to carry out some common purpose.

Under the Public Order Decree No. 5 of 1979 the Governor of each State is vested with power to direct the conduct of assemblies, meetings and processions on public roads or places of public resort in the State. Assembly in the Decree is defined as a meeting of five or more persons. The Decree allows the Governor to delegate his powers to appropriate police officers. All persons taking part in an assembly forbidden by the Decree are guilty of an offence punishable with a fine of one thousand naira or imprisonment for six months or both.

Affray

Any person who takes part in a fight in a public place is guilty of affray. It is a misdemeanour and the offender is liable to imprisonment for one year. To secure conviction, the prosecution must prove that the fight took place in a public place. It is not sufficient, for instance, to prove that the fight took place at a general hospital.

In some cases, the law allows a person to use force in defending himself against an attack or in order to affect some other lawful purpose. If a fight occurs in such circumstances the person using force is not guilty of an offence.

The Code does not require that the fight should be to the terror of any person. A person using force in self-defence or in other circumstances where the use of force is lawful is not guilty of the offence of affray.

CHAPTER 5

Corruption and Abuse of Office

Disclosure of Official Secrets

Any person who being employed in the public service, publishes or communicates any fact which comes to his knowledge by virtue of his office, and which it is his duty to keep secret, or any document which comes to his possession by virtue of his office and which it is his duty to keep secret, except to some person to whom he is bound to publish or communicate it, is guilty of a misdemeanour, and is liable to imprisonment for two years.

Any person who being employed in the public service, without proper authority abstracts, or makes a copy of, any document the property of his employer is guilty of a misdemeanour and is liable to imprisonment for one year.

A prosecution for an offence under the provisions of this section shall not be commenced except by, or with the consent of, a law officer.

Official Corruption

Any person who:

(1) being employed in the public service and being charged with the performance of any duty by virtue of such employment, not being a duty touching the administration of justice, corruptly asks, receives or obtains, or agrees or attempts to receive or obtain, any property or benefit of any kind for himself or any other person on account of anything already done or omitted to be done, or be afterwards done or omitted to be done, by himself in the discharge of the duties of his office; or

(2) corruptly gives, confers or procures or promises or offers to give or confer, or to procure or attempts to procure, to, upon, or for, any person employed in the public service or to, upon, or for, any other person, any property or benefit, of any kind on account of any such act or omission on the part of the peace officer or other person so employed; is guilty of a felony, and is liable to imprisonment for seven years.

The mischief aimed at by the above provision is the receiving or offering of some benefit, regard or inducement to sway or deflect a person employed in the public service from the honest and impartial discharge of his duties – in other words as a bribe for corruption or corrupt practice or its price.

The officials of the Nigerian Arts Authority and of Nigerian Railway Corporation are deemed to be persons employed in the public service for the purpose of this provision. A person who knowingly acts as a go-between in the payment of a bribe is an accomplice of the receiver as well as the giver.

Corruption may be divided into **official corruption** and **judicial corruption.** Official corruption is related to public office while judicial corruption touches the administration of justice. A public officer who does not do any job touching the administration of justice cannot be charged with judicial corruption otherwise the conviction shall be upset. On the other hand an officer engaged in a judicial office cannot be charged with corruption in matters touching the administration of justice.

Where a police constable was induced by a bribe of £5 not to prosecute an offender for forgery it was held that the duty to prosecute an offender is clearly a duty touching the administration of justice. The offender was therefore guilty of judicial corruption and not official corruption.

But where the duty of a policeman was the renewal of driving licences, he was rightly convicted of official corruption because the renewal of driving licences, clearly did not touch the administration of justice.

The expression "administration of justice" is not limited to the hearing of cases whether civil or criminal in the courts. It includes steps taken preliminary to the hearing of cases. In criminal matters it starts with the complaint by the complainant at the police station to officers whose duty is to hear and investigate such complaints with a view to deciding whether the person against whom the complaints are made should be arrested or summoned. A police constable who demanded £2 and some beer in order to refrain from prosecuting an offender was therefore guilty of judicial corruption.

Judicial Corruption

Any person who:

(a) being a judicial officer, corruptly asks, receives, or obtains or agrees or attempts to receive or obtain, any property or benefit of any kind for himself or any other person on account of anything already done or omitted to be done or to be afterwards done or omitted to be done, by him in his judicial capacity, or

(b) corruptly gives, confers, or procures, or promises or offers to give or confer or to procure or to, upon, or for, any other person, any property or benefit of any kind on account of any such act or omission on the part of such judicial officer; is guilty of a felony, and is liable to imprisonment for fourteen years.

The offender cannot be arrested without warrant. The term "Judicial Officer" includes a member of a native tribunal, an arbitrator or umpire, and any person appointed to act as a commissioner under the Commission of Inquiry Act. The acts done by a judicial officer in his judicial capacity includes not only acts done in the course of hearing and determining a cause or matter, including any preliminary or interlocutory proceedings, but any acts of such a kind that, if they were done by an inferior court, they would be subject to appeal or to *certiorari*.

'Judicial proceeding' includes any proceeding had or taken in or before any court, tribunal, Commission of Inquiry, or person, in which evidence may be taken on oath or in or before a native tribunal whether such tribunal takes evidence on oath or not.

Any person who accepts reward to influence members of native tribunals is guilty of a misdemeanour and is liable to imprisonment for two years.

Any person who being a peace officer not acting judicially or being a person employed in the public service in any capacity not judicial for the prosecution or detention or punishment of offenders, corruptly asks, receives or obtains or agrees or attempts to receive or obtain, any property or benefit is guilty of a felony and is liable to imprisonment for fourteen years.

The administration of justice is not limited to the hearing of cases whether civil or criminal in the courts. It includes steps taken preliminary to the hearing of cases.

Extortion by Public Officers

Any person who, being employed in the public service, takes, or accepts from any person, for the performance of his duty as such officer, any reward beyond his proper pay and emoluments or any promise of such reward is guilty of a felony, and is liable to imprisonment for three years.

It is a misdemeanour for public officers to receive property to show favour. Such public officer is liable to imprisonment for six months. It is an offence of official corruption for a public officer to invite or receive bribes on account of his own duties. This offence is a felony punishable with seven years imprisonment.

Similarly any public officer who gives bribes on account of his duties is guilty of a felony punishable with seven years imprisonment. A public officer who acquires a private interest in any contract with respect to a matter in the department of the service in which he is employed is guilty of a felony and is liable to imprisonment for three years.

Impersonating a public officer is a felony punishable with three years imprisonment. Impersonating a soldier or police officer is a misdemeanour punishable with one year imprisonment. Any person who:

(1) publicly offers a reward for the return of any property which has been stolen or lost, and in the offer makes use of any words purporting that no questions will be asked, or that the person producing such property will not be seized or molested; or

(2) publicly offers to return to any person who may have bought or advanced money by way of loan upon any stolen or lost property the money so paid or advanced, or any other sum of money or reward for the return of such property; or

(3) prints or publishes any such offer;

is guilty of a simple offence, and is liable to a fine of one hundred naira.

CHAPTER 6

Offences Relating to the Administration of Justice

Perjury

Any person who commits perjury is liable to imprisonment for fourteen years. If the offender committed the offence in order to procure the conviction of another person for an offence punishable with death or with imprisonment for life he is liable to imprisonment for life.

Any person who, in any judicial proceeding, or for the purpose of instituting any judicial proceeding, knowingly gives false testimony touching any matter which is material to any question pending in that proceeding or intending to be raised in that proceeding, is guilty of an offence, which is called perjury.

It is immaterial whether the testimony is given on oath or under any other sanction authorised by law. The forms and ceremonies used in administering the oath or in otherwise binding the person giving the testimony to speak the truth are immaterial, if he assents to the forms and ceremonies actually used. The offence of perjury is committed whether the false testimony is given orally or in writing.

It is not a defence that the court or tribunal is not properly constituted or is not held in the proper place, if it actually acts as a court or tribunal in the proceeding in which the testimony is given. It is immaterial whether the person who gives the testimony is a competent witness or not, or whether the testimony is admissible in the proceeding or not.

A person cannot be convicted of committing perjury, or of counselling or procuring the commission of perjury upon the uncorroborated testimony of one witness. It must be shown that the false testimony was given knowingly and not by inadvertence or mistake.

The offender cannot be arrested without warrant.

A clerk had previously been charged with stealing some drums of petrol. During the trial he was asked if he was the owner of a particular car. He denied ownership of the car but in fact he was the owner. He was charged with perjury and it was argued in his favour that the false statement was not material in the proceeding. The statement was held material because if he had admitted ownership of the car, the prosecution would have asked him to explain how he could afford to buy a car. The accused was thus convicted.

Fabrication of Evidence

Fabrication of evidence is a felony punishable with seven years imprisonment. Any person who procures any person called or to be called as a witness to give false testimony or withhold true testimony is guilty of a felony and is liable to imprisonment for seven years. This offence can only be committed when judicial proceedings are in existence, not while a complaint is still being investigated by police.

Deceit of witnesses and destruction of evidence are felonies each of which is punishable with three years imprisonment. It is a misdemeanour punishable with one year imprisonment to prevent witnesses from attending court or tribunal to give evidence. Perverting justice is a felony and the offender is liable to imprisonment for seven years. It is a felony to compound or conceal a felony. If the felony is such that a person convicted of it is liable to be sentenced to death or imprisonment for life, the offender is guilty of a felony and is liable to imprisonment for seven years. In any other case, the offender is liable to imprisonment for three years.

Contempt of Court

Any person who:

(1) within premises in which any judicial proceeding is being

had or taken or within the precinct of the same shows disrespect, in speech or manner, to or with reference to such proceeding is being had or taken, or

(2) having been called upon to give evidence in a judicial proceeding, fails to attend or having attended refuses to be sworn or to make an affirmation, or, having been sworn or affirmed, refuses without lawful excuse to answer a question, or to produce document or prevarication, or remains in the room in which such proceeding is being had and taken, after the witnesses have been ordered to leave such room, or

(3) while, a judicial proceeding is pending, makes use of any speech or writing, misrepresenting such proceeding, or capable of prejudicing any people in favour of or against any party to such proceeding or calculated to lower the authority of any person before whom such proceeding is being had or taken, or

(4) causes an obstruction or disturbance in the course of a judicial proceeding, or

(5) publishes a report of the evidence taken in any judicial proceeding which had been directed to be held in private, or

(6) attempts wrongly to interfere with or influence a witness in a judicial proceeding, either before or after he has given evidence, in connection with such evidence, or

(7) dismisses a servant because he has given evidence on behalf of a certain party to a judicial proceeding, or

(8) retakes possession of land from any person who has recently obtained possession by writ of court, or

(9) commits any other act of intentional disrespect to any judicial proceeding or to any person whom such proceeding is being had or taken,

is guilty of a simple offence and is liable to imprisonment for three years.

The essence of contempt of court is action or inaction amounting to interference with or obstruction to, or having a tendency to interfere with or obstruct the due administration of justice. Such conduct may be punishable either summarily under the inherent powers possessed by all courts of record to prevent abuse of their own procedure, or under the provision of the Criminal Code.

A person cannot be punished both under the inherent power of the court and under the provision of the Criminal Code.

Paragraph (1) above covers the case of contempt in the face of the court while paragraph (2) covers the case of a person who refuses to obey the instruction of the court. Paragraph (9) is an omnibus paragraph which sweeps up any other cases not coming within the preceding paragraphs.

Obstructing Officers of Court of Justice

Any person who wilfully obstructs or resists any person lawfully charged with the execution of an order or warrant of any court, is guilty of a misdemeanour and is liable to imprisonment for one year, or to a fine of two hundred naira.

CHAPTER 7

Offences Against Morality

Unnatural Offences

Any person who:

(1) has carnal knowledge of any person against the order of nature, or

(2) has carnal knowledge of an animal, or

(3) permits a male person to have carnal knowledge of him or her against the order of nature;

is guilty of a felony, and is liable to imprisonment for fourteen years. An attempt to commit this offence is a felony and the offender is liable to imprisonment for seven years.

Indecent Treatment of Boys Under the Age of Fourteen Years

This is a felony punishable with seven years imprisonment. Indecent practices between males is a felony and the offence is punishable with three years imprisonment. This provision is extremely wide in its scope and would appear to cover all kinds of indecent or lewd practices between male persons.

Defilement of Girls Under Thirteen Years

Any person who has unlawful carnal knowledge of a girl under the age of thirteen years is guilty of felony, and is liable to imprisonment for life with or without whipping. An attempt to commit this offence is punishable with fourteen years imprisonment with or without whipping.

Prosecution for the full offence or the attempt must be begun within two months after the offence is committed. A person cannot be convicted of either of the offences upon the uncorroborated testimony of one witness. In some states in Nigeria, the reference is to a girl under the age of eleven not thirteen years.

Procuration

Any person who:

(1)   procures a girl or woman who is under the age of eighteen years and is not a common prostitute or of known immoral character, to have unlawful carnal connection with any other person or persons either in Nigeria or elsewhere, or

(2)   procures a woman or girl to become a common prostitute either in Nigeria or elsewhere, or

(3)   procures a woman or girl to leave Nigeria with intent that she may become an inmate of a brothel elsewhere, or

(4)   procures a woman or girl to leave her usual place of abode in Nigeria, such place not being a brothel, with intent that she may, for the purpose of prostitution, become an inmate of a brothel either in Nigeria or elsewhere;
is guilty of a misdemeanour, and is liable to imprisonment for two years.

A person cannot be convicted of any of the offences in this section upon the uncorroborated testimony of one witness.

Persons Trading in Prostitution

Every male person who:

(a)   knowingly lives wholly or in part on the earnings of prostitution, or

(b)   in any public place persistently solicits or importunates for immoral purposes;
shall be liable to imprisonment for two years, and in the case of a second or subsequent conviction, shall in addition

to any term of imprisonment awarded be liable to whipping.

Every female who is proved to have for the purposes of gain exercised control, direction or influence over the movements of a prostitute in such a manner as to show that she is aiding, abetting or compelling her prostitution with any person or generally shall be liable to imprisonment for two years.

Keeping a Brothel

Whoever:

(a) keeps or manages or assists in the management of a brothel; or

(b) being the tenant, lessee, or occupier or person in charge of any premises, knowingly permits such premises or any part thereof to be used as a brothel or for the purposes of habitual prostitution; or

(c) being the lessor or landlord of any premises, or the agent or such lessor or landlord, lets the same or any part thereof with the knowledge that such premises or some part thereof are or is to be used as brothel, or is wilfully a party to the continued use of such premises or any part thereof as a brothel, shall be liable –

    (i)   to a fine of one hundred naira or to imprisonment for six months, and

    (ii)   on a second or subsequent conviction, to a fine of three hundred naira or to imprisonment for one year; or in either case, to both fine and imprisonment.

CHAPTER 8

Idle and Disorderly Persons, Rogues and Vagabonds

Idle and Disorderly Persons

The following persons –

(a) every common prostitute:

   (i)   behaving in a disorderly or indecent manner in any public place;

   (ii)   loitering and persisting, importuning or soliciting persons for the purpose of prostitution;

(b) every person wandering or placing himself in any public place to beg or gather alms, or causing or procuring or encouraging any child or children so to do;

(c) every person playing at any game of chance for money or money's worth in any public place; and

(d) every person who, in any public place, conducts himself in a manner likely to cause a breach of the peace;

   shall be deemed idle and disorderly persons and may be guilty of a simple offence, and shall be liable to imprisonment for one month.

Rogues and Vagabonds

The following persons –

(i) every person convicted of any offence under the last preceding section after having been previously convicted as an idle and disorderly person;

(ii) every person wandering abroad and endeavouring by the exposure of wounds or deformation to obtain or gather alms,

(iii) every person going about as a gatherer or collector of alms, or endeavouring to procure charitable contributions of any nature or kind, under any false or fraudulent pretence,

(iv) every suspected person or reputed thief who has no visible means of subsistence and cannot give a good account of himself,

(v) every person who exercises control, direction or influence over the movements of a prostitute in such a manner as to show that he is aiding, abetting or controlling her prostitution with any man, whether a particular man or not,

(vi) every person found wandering in or upon or near any premises or in any road or highway or any place adjacent thereto or in any public place at such time under such circumstances as to lead to the conclusion that such person is there for an illegal or disorderly purpose;

shall be deemed to be a rouge and vagabond and is guilty of a misdemeanour, and is liable on summary conviction for the first offence to imprisonment for one year. An offender may be arrested without warrant.

Escapes and Rescues

Rescues

(1) Any person who by force rescues or attempts to rescue from lawful custody any other person –

(a) is, if such last-named person is under sentence of death or penal servitude or imprisonment for life, or charged with an offence punishable with death, or penal servitude or imprisonment for life, guilty of a felony, and is liable to imprisonment for life; and

(b) is, in any other case, guilty of a felony, is liable to imprisonment for seven years.

(2) If the person rescued is in the custody of a private person, the offender must have notice of the fact that the person rescued is in such custody.

Escapes

Any person who, being in lawful custody, escapes from such custody – is, if he is charged with or has been convicted of, felony or misdemeanour guilty of a felony and is liable to imprisonment for seven years, with or without whipping.

In any other case, the offender is guilty of a misdemeanour and is liable to imprisonment for two years. It is immaterial whether force is used to effect the escape or not. Any person who aids a prisoner in escaping or attempting to escape from lawful custody, or facilitates the escape is guilty of a felony, and is liable to imprisonment for seven years.

If a prisoner escapes through the negligence of a prison or police officer, the latter is guilty of a misdemeanour punishable with two years imprisonment.

CHAPTER 9

Assaults and Violence to the Person Generally

Definition of Assault

A person who strikes, touches, or moves or otherwise applies force of any kind to the person of another, either directly or indirectly without his consent or with his consent if the consent is obtained by fraud or who by any bodily act or gesture attempts or threatens to apply force of any kind to the person of another without his consent, in such circumstances that the person making the attempt or threat has actually or apparently a present ability to effect his purpose, is said to assault that other person and the act is called an assault.

The term "applies force" includes the case of applying heat, light, electricity, force, gas, odour, or any other substance or thing whatever, if applied in such a degree as to cause injury or personal discomfort.

An assault is unlawful and constitutes an offence unless it is authorised or justified or excused by law. The application of force by one person to the person of another may be unlawful, although it is done with the consent of that other person.

Any person who unlawfully assaults another is guilty of a misdemeanour and is liable if no greater punishment is provided to imprisonment for one year.

Any person who assaults another with intent to have carnal knowledge of him or her against the order of nature is guilty of a felony, and is liable to imprisonment for fourteen years. Any person who unlawfully and indecently assaults any male person is guilty of a felony, and is liable to imprisonment for three years. The offender cannot be arrested without warrant.

39

Any person who unlawfully assaults and uses actual violence on a peace officer or any other person while acting in the execution of his duty in or concerning the preservation of a vessel in distress or of any vessel or goods wrecked or standing or lying under water is guilty of a felony, and is liable to imprisonment for seven years.

Any person who unlawfully assaults another and thereby does him harm is guilty of a felony, and is liable to imprisonment for three years.

Consent negates the offence of assault. But consent obtained by the use of threat or intimidation is not valid consent. Nor is consent obtained by fraud a valid consent because fraud vitiates consent.

Provocation is a valid defence to a charge of assault. The characteristics of provocation reducing a charge of murder to manslaughter are similar to provocation as a defence to a charge of assault.

Serious Assaults

Any person who:

(i)   assaults another with intent to commit a felony or with intent to resist or prevent lawful arrest or detention of himself or of any other person, or

(ii)   assaults, resists or wilfully obstructs a police officer while acting in the execution of his duty or any person acting in aid of a police officer while so acting, or

(iii) unlawfully assaults, resists or obstructs any person engaged in the lawful execution of any process against any property or in making a lawful distress while so engaged, or

(iv)   assaults, resists or obstructs any person engaged in such lawful distress, with intent to rescue any property lawfully taken under such process or distress, or

(v)   assaults any person on account of any act done by him in the execution of any duty imposed on him by law, or

(vi) assaults any person in pursuance of any unlawful conspiracy respecting any manufacture, trade, business or occupation or respecting any person or persons concerned or employed in any manufacture, trade, business or occupation, or the wages of any such person or persons;

is guilty of a felony, and is liable to imprisonment for three years.

Obstruction implies something less than assault and other than resistance and extends to acts done to interfere with constables who are acting in the execution of their duty.

Assault on Females – Rape and Abduction

Rape

Any person who has unlawful carnal knowledge of a woman or girl, without her consent, or with her consent, if the consent is obtained by force or by means of threats or intimidation of any kind, or by fear of harm, or by means of false and fraudulent representation as to the nature of the act, or, in the case of a married woman, by impersonating her husband, is guilty of an offence which is called rape. Any person who commits the offence of rape is liable to imprisonment for life, with or without whipping.

Rape is complete upon proof of penetration. A husband cannot be guilty of rape on his wife but he may be guilty of wounding, doing grievous harm or assault. Where a man has sex with a woman while asleep, the man is guilty of rape. The fact that the woman raped is a common prostitute is no excuse, although in such cases a court may be unwilling to believe that the woman did not give her consent. Attempt to commit rape is a felony and the offender is liable to imprisonment for fourteen years, with or without whipping.

Any person who unlawfully and indecently assaults a woman or girl is guilty of a misdemeanour and is liable to imprisonment for two years.

Since a male person under the age of 12 is presumed to be incapable of having carnal knowledge, he cannot be guilty of rape or attempted rape. He may however be found guilty of indecent assault. The offence of rape cannot be committed without penetration. It is no excuse that the complainant is the accused's concubine. If, the woman consents, there is no rape. But consent obtained by force or by threats or intimidation is no consent. Consent given because of exhaustion after persistent struggle is no consent.

In a decided case, the accused entered a lady's room uninvited, took off his clothes, expressed a desire to have sexual intercourse with her and actually caught hold of her. It was held that these facts did not constitute the offence of attempted rape because they merely indicated that the accused wanted to have and had made preparation to have intercourse with the complainant.

Abduction

Any person who, with intent to marry or carnally know a female of any age or to cause her to be married or carnally known by any other person, takes her away, or detains her, against her will, is guilty of a felony, and is liable to imprisonment for seven years.

CHAPTER 10

Homicide

Murder

Any person who unlawfully kills another is guilty of an offence which is called murder or manslaughter, according to the circumstances of the case. Except as hereinafter set forth a person who unlawfully kills another under any of the following circumstances, that is:

(i)   if the offender intends to cause death of the person killed, or that of some other person;

(ii) if the offender intends to do to that person killed or to some other persons some grievous harm;

(iii) if the death is by means of any act done in the prosecution of an unlawful purpose, which act is of such nature as to be likely to endanger human life;

(iv) if the offender intends to do grievous harm to some person for the purpose of facilitating the commission of an offence which is such that the offender may be arrested without warrant, or for the purpose of facilitating the flight of an offender who has committed or attempted to commit any such offence;

(v)   if death is caused by administering any stupefying or overpowering things for either of the purpose last aforesaid;

(vi) if the death is caused by wilfully stopping the breath of any person for either of such purposes;

is guilty of murder.

In the second case ((ii) above) it is immaterial that the offender did not intend to hurt the particular person who is killed.

In the third case ((iii) above) it is immaterial that the offender did not intend to hurt any person.

In the last three cases ((iv)(v)(vi) above) it is immaterial that the offender did not intend to cause death or did not know that death was likely to result.

A person is not deemed to have killed another, if the death of that other person does not take place within a year and a day of the cause of death.

The burden of proving that the accused person caused the death of the deceased is on the prosecution. The cause of death or the omission which caused death must be traced to the accused. In a decided case, the accused administered an injection to the deceased who died as a result of an infection which could have been caused by the injection or by germs of the body of the deceased. The accused was acquitted because it was not shown how the infection was caused. It was held that the cause of death was not proved.

In another case, the accused beat the deceased with a stick and left him lying on the ground injured. The deceased was taken to the hospital where he died after two days illness. This was held not sufficient proof that the accused caused the death of the deceased because it has not been shown that the deceased died of injuries inflicted by the accused.

But in a case were the accused stabbed the deceased twice and it was proved that the stabs were in the stomach and back and the deceased died two days after receiving these injuries, it was held that it was proper for the court to infer the cause of death from the circumstances. In the latter case there was no medical evidence as to the cause of death.

On a charge of murder, the fact that the corpse is not found is immaterial because death is a fact which can be proved by circumstantial evidence. But the circumstantial evidence must be such as to render the commission of the crime certain.

Homicide may be lawful or excusable in the following circumstances:

1. **Legal execution:** where an executioner is authorised to execute a condemned criminal.

2. **Self-defence:** This defence is not open to an abnormally nervous or excitable person who on being assailed by a comparatively minor assault kills his assailant.

3. **Aiding in self-defence:** It was held that this defence availed the accused who having observed the deceased inflict a fatal matchet cut on one of his (accused's) sons and cut the other on the knee with the matchet, snatched the matchet from the deceased and killed him.

4. **Defence of property:** In a decided case, the accused was attacked in his house. Stones were thrown at the house which almost ruined it. At first he remained in the house, but after a time, being exasperated, he took his brother's gun, fired at the crowd and killed someone. On a charge of murder it was held that the accused was entitled to be acquitted on the ground that the killing was justifiable in defence of his property.

5. **Death by misadventure:** This occurs where a person kills another in purely accidental circumstances without intending to cause death or unlawful harm and without gross negligence.

6. **Killing of thieves:** A person may kill an escaping thief provided he uses reasonable force to overcome any force used by the thief in resisting arrest. But generally there is no law which authorises the killing of a person merely because he is a notorious thief or because he is caught stealing.

7. **Suppression of riot:** Any person may lawfully kill in order to suppress a riot provided that the danger to be apprehended from the continuance of the riot warrants such killing.

8. **Consent to death:** Consent by a person to the causing of his own death does not affect criminal responsibility of any person by whom such death is caused. In a decided case, the accused, a native doctor prepared some charms for the deceased. The deceased then invited the accused to test the charms on him by firing a shot at him. The accused shot

him in the chest and killed him. He was convicted of murder.

9. **Provocation:** No amount of provocation can ever justify a killing. The most that it can do is to reduce murder to manslaughter. For this to happen the provocation must be such as can cause a reasonable person to lose his self-control. It must be proved that the accused did in fact lose his self-control. The act, which causes death must be done in the heat of passion caused by sudden provocation and before there is time for passion to cool. Provocation by one person is no excuse for killing another person who does not in fact offer any provocation to the accused. Provocation may be by words or deed.

Manslaughter

A person who unlawfully kills another in such circumstances as not to constitute murder is guilty of manslaughter. Any killing which is neither authorised nor justified nor excused by law, and yet which does not amount to murder is manslaughter.

If a person dies as a result of negligent driving of a motor vehicle, the driver may be guilty of manslaughter depending on the circumstances of the case. Where the driver of a vehicle, in trying to avoid a child, struck and killed two other persons, and where he was not driving at an excessive speed, it was held that this was not manslaughter.

There is no rule that if an accident occurs the driver is guilty unless he explains the accident to the satisfaction of the court. If a driver has the necessary skill, the fact that he has no driving licence is not evidence of reckless or dangerous driving on his part. It is gross negligence on the part of a driver who drives fast and zig-zags along the road in a built-up area. He is guilty of manslaughter if he kills any person by such negligent driving. Excessive speed in itself would not be conclusive evidence of criminal negligence, but it may be strong evidence of dangerous driving.

Apart from driving of motor vehicles, where an act of the defendant contains the elements of criminal negligence and death results the offence of manslaughter is created. When a person who unlawfully kills another in circumstances which but for the provisions of this section, would constitute murder does the act which causes death in the heat of passion caused by sudden provocation and before there is time for his passion to cool off, he is guilty of manslaughter only.

Murder is punishable by death while manslaughter is punishable by imprisonment for life. Attempted murder is punishable by life imprisonment. Although the law says that manslaughter and attempted murder are punishable by life imprisonment, another provision of the law gives a judge the discretion to inflict a lower punishment.

CHAPTER 11

Stealing and Like Offences

Stealing

Any person who fraudulently takes anything capable of being stolen, or fraudulently converts to his own use or to the use of any other person anything capable of being stolen is said to steal that thing. Land cannot be stolen. An ownerless property cannot be stolen. A thing may be ownerless because it is incapable of being owned at all or because it is abandoned. A corpse cannot be the subject of ownership and therefore cannot be stolen.

A person who takes or converts anything capable of being stolen is deemed to do so fraudulently if he does so with any of the following intents:

(a) an intent permanently to deprive the owner of the thing of it;

(b) an intent permanently to deprive any person who has special property in the thing of such property;

(c) an intent to use the thing as a pledge or security;

(d) an intent to part with it on a condition as to its return which the person taking or converting it may be unable to perform;

(e) an intent to deal with it in such a manner that it cannot be returned in the condition in which it was at the time of the taking or conversion.

(f) in the case of money an intent to use it at the will of the person who takes or converts it, although he may intend afterwards to repay the amount to the owner.

A defendant collected money from certain persons as deposit for sending them to America on scholarship. He did not send them and did not refund their money on demand or at a reasonable time thereafter. He was convicted of stealing under paragraph (f) above.

In another case the accused received a loan from a Housing Corporation to build a house on a piece of land which he mortgaged to the Corporation. He used the money instead to contest an election. He was convicted of stealing because the money still belonged to the Corporation until he used it for the specific purpose for which he received it. It made no difference that he might have intended to repay afterwards. The taking or conversion may be fraudulent, although it is affected without secrecy or attempt at concealment.

A person shall not be deemed to take a thing unless he moves the thing or causes it to move. If the property is taken without the owner's consent the act is stealing notwithstanding that it was done openly, and if the property is converted without the owner's consent the act is stealing even if done openly or that the original taking was done without fraudulent intent.

The test of stealing is what was the intent of the accused at the time of the taking or conversion. If money deposited for a specific purpose is neither used for that purpose nor returned on demand or at a reasonable time thereafter, stealing could have been committed. A credit customer who received goods, omitted to sign the invoices and later denied receiving them had taken them fraudulently and was guilty of stealing.

An owner may be guilty of stealing his own property. There are cases of stealing where the true owner consents to the thief having possession of the goods but not to his stealing them. The distinction between theft and obtaining by deception is that in theft the owner means at most to part with the possession of the property, whereas in obtaining by deception he is induced by fraud to agree to part with the ownership as well as possession.

Stealing by Persons Having an Interest in the Thing Stolen
When any person takes or converts anything capable of being stolen in such circumstances as would otherwise amount to stealing, it is immaterial that he himself has a special property or

interest therein, or that he himself is the owner of the thing taken or converted subject to some special property or interest of some other person therein, or that he is lessee of the thing, or that he himself is one of two or more joint owners of the thing; or that he is a director or officer of a Corporation or Company or Society who are the owners of it.

Husband and Wife
A person who, while a man and his wife are living together, procures either of them to deal with anything which is, to his knowledge, the property of the other in a manner which would be stealing if they were not married, is deemed to have stolen the thing and may be charged with stealing it. The husband and wife of Christian marriage cannot, in ordinary circumstances steal one another's property.

Punishment of Stealing
Any person who steals anything capable of being stolen is guilty of a felony and is liable if no other punishment is provided to imprisonment for three years.

1. If the thing stolen is a testamentary instrument whether the testator is living or dead, the offender is liable to imprisonment for life.
2. If the thing stolen is postal matter or any chattel, money or valuable security contained in any postal matter, the offender is liable to imprisonment for life.
3. If the thing stolen is any of the things following, that is; a horse, ass, mule, camel, bull, cow, ox, ram, ewe, wether, goat or pig, or the young of any such animal, the offender is liable to imprisonment for seven years.
4. If the offence is committed in any of the following circumstances:
    (a)   if the thing is stolen from the person of another;
    (b)   if the thing is stolen in a dwelling-house, and its value exceeds ten naira, or the offender at or

immediately before or after the time of stealing uses or threatens to use violence to any person in the dwelling-house;

(c) if the thing is stolen from any kind of vessel or vehicle or place of deposit used for the conveyance or custody of goods in transit from one place to another;

(d) if the thing stolen is attached to or forms part of a railway;

(e) if the thing is stolen from a vessel which is in distress or wrecked or stranded;

(f) if the thing is stolen from a public office in which it is deposited or kept;

(g) if the offender, in order to commit the offence opens any locked room, box or other receptacle, by means of a key or other instrument;

the offender is liable to imprisonment for seven years.

5. If the offender is a person employed in the public service and the thing stolen is the property of the State, or came into the possession of the offender by virtue of his employment, he is liable to imprisonment for seven years.

6. If the offender is a clerk or servant, and the thing stolen is the property of his employer, or came into the possession of the offender on account of his employer, he is liable to imprisonment for seven years.

7. If the offender is a director or officer of a Corporation or Company and the thing stolen is the property of the Corporation or the Company, he is liable to imprisonment for seven years.

8. If the thing stolen is any of the following things:

(a) property which has been received by the offender with a power of attorney for the disposition thereof;

(b) property which has been entrusted to the offender either alone or jointly with any other person for him

to retain in safe custody or to apply, pay or deliver
for any purpose or to any person the same or any part
thereof or any proceeds thereof;

(c)   property which has been received by the offender
either alone or jointly with any other person for or on
account of any other person;

(d)   the whole or part of the proceeds of any valuable
security which has been received by the offender
with a direction that the proceeds thereof should be
applied to any purpose or paid to any person
specified in the direction;

(e)   the whole or part of the proceeds arising from any
disposition of any property which has been received
by the offender by virtue of a power of attorney for
such disposition, such power of attorney having been
received by the offender with a direction that such
proceeds should be applied to any purpose or paid to
any person specified in the direction;

the offender is liable to imprisonment for seven years.

9.   If the thing stolen is of the value of one thousand naira or
more, the offender is liable to imprisonment for seven
years.

10.   If the thing stolen is a fixture or chattel let to the offender to
be used by him with a house or lodging, and its value
exceeds ten naira, he is liable to imprisonment for seven
years.

11.   If the offender, before committing the offence had been
convicted of any of the felonies or misdemeanours defined
in the Criminal Code, he is liable to imprisonment for seven
years.

Concealing Wills

Any person who with intent to defraud, conceals any
testamentary instrument whether the testator is living or dead, is

guilty of a felony and is liable to imprisonment for fourteen years.

Robbery

Any person who steals anything, and, at or immediately before or immediately after the time of stealing it, uses or threatens to use actual violence to any person or property in order to obtain or retain the thing stolen or to prevent or overcome resistance to its being stolen or retained, is said to be guilty of robbery. This offence is punishable by imprisonment for fourteen years.

If the offender is armed with any dangerous or offensive weapon or instrument, or is in company with one or more other person or persons, or if, at or immediately before or immediately after the time of the robbery, he wounds or uses any other personal violence to any person, he is liable to imprisonment for life with or without whipping. Robbery is stealing accompanied by the use of threat or actual violence to any person or property.

Any person who assaults another person with intent to steal anything, and at or immediately before or immediately after the time of the assault, uses or threatens to use actual violence to any person or property in order to obtain the thing intended to be stolen or to prevent or overcome resistance to its being stolen is guilty of a felony, that is, attempted robbery and, is liable to imprisonment for life with or without whipping.

Any person who assaults any person with intent to steal anything is guilty of a felony, and is liable to imprisonment for three years.

In a case of robbery, if it is proved that the offender is armed with any dangerous or offensive weapon, or is in company with one or more other person or persons, or wounds, or uses personal violence to any person, he is liable to imprisonment for life with or without whipping under the Robbery and Firearms (Special Provisions) Decree No. 47 of 1970.

The offence of robbery under the Decree is punishable with imprisonment for not less than 21 years. If the offender is armed with any firearms or any offensive weapon or is in company with any person so armed, or at or immediately after the time of the robbery he wounds any person the punishment under the Decree is death which is executed by hanging or by firing squad.

Attempted robbery is punishable by imprisonment for not less than 14 years but not more than 21 years. If the offender is armed with any firearms or offensive weapon, the punishment is imprisonment for life with whipping which shall not exceed 24 strokes.

Any person who aids, counsels, abets, procures or conspires with any person to commit robbery or attempted robbery is guilty of the offence as a principal offender and is liable to be proceeded against and punished under the Decree.

Burglary

A person who breaks any part, whether external or internal of a building, or opens by unlocking, pulling, pushing, lifting, or any other means whatever any door, window, shutter, celler flap, or other thing, intended to close or cover an opening in a building, or an opening giving passage from one part of a building to another, is said to break the building;

A person is said to enter a building as soon as any part of his body or any part of any instrument used by him is within the building.

A person who obtains entrance into a building by means of any threat or artifice used for that purpose, or by collusion with any person in the building, or who enters any chimney or other aperture of the building permanently left open for any necessary purpose, but not intended to be ordinarily used as a means of entrance is deemed to have broken and entered the building.

House -Breaking

Any person who:

(1) breaks and enters the dwelling-house of another with intent to commit a felony therein; or

(2) having entered the dwelling-house of another with intent to commit a felony therein or having committed a felony in the dwelling-house of another;

is guilty of a felony, and is liable to imprisonment for fourteen years.

If the offence is committed in the night, the offender is liable to imprisonment for life.

To constitute an offence of house-breaking there must be breaking either actual or constructive. Breaking does not extend to the opening of cupboard door and the like.

Entering a dwelling-house with intent to commit felony or breaking into a building and committing a felony therein is punishable in the case of entering with seven years imprisonment. But if the offence is committed in the night, the offender is liable to imprisonment for fourteen years. In the case of breaking into a dwelling-house, the offender is guilty of a felony and is liable to imprisonment for fourteen years.

Any person who breaks and enters a school, house, shop, warehouse, store, office, or counting-house or a building which is adjacent to a dwelling-house and occupied it but is not part of it with intent to commit a felony therein, is guilty of a felony, and is liable to imprisonment for seven years.

Any person who breaks and enters a building ordinarily used for religious worship and commits a felony therein or having committed felony in any such building breaks out of it, is guilty of a felony, and is liable to imprisonment for fourteen years.

Obtaining by False Pretence

Any representation made by words, writing or conduct of a matter of fact either past or present which representation is false in fact, and which the person making it knows to be false or does not believe to be true, is a false pretence.

Obtaining Goods by False Pretence

Any person who by any false pretence, and with intent to defraud, obtains from any other person anything capable of being stolen or induces any other person to deliver to any person anything capable of being stolen, is guilty of a felony, and is liable to imprisonment for three years. It is immaterial that the thing is obtained or its delivery is induced through the medium of a contract induced by the false pretence. The offender cannot be arrested without warrant unless found committing the offence.

This is the offence popularly called **419** because it is contained in Section 419 of the Criminal Code Act. The section covers not only goods but also anything capable of being stolen. A person who orders and eats a meal in a restaurant does not automatically make any representation as to his ability to pay; though the wearing of some distinctive form of dress to which the accused was not entitled might be sufficient pretence. A pretence as to future conduct is not within the section; thus a charge which alleges the obtaining of a sum of money by a false pretence that the accused will use the money for a particular purpose discloses no offence. A pretence that the accused had a job which he was in a position to offer comes under this section. It is no defence that the person defrauded parted with his money in order that it might be put to an unlawful purpose. Where the accused having a genuine claim, fraudulently exaggerates the amount of his claim, he may be convicted of obtaining the excess by false pretences.

In one case, the accused pretending to be a clerk of a store helped a customer to purchase some goods from the store. The customer gave him the price he mentioned which was in fact more than the price of the goods. The accused pocketed the difference. He was convicted of stealing and not obtaining goods by false pretence.

In another case, the accused a county council revenue collector was issued with a revenue collector's receipt book for the collection of fees for bicycle licences. He forged a similar receipt book with which he collected fees and misappropriated the money received. It was held that the offence was false pretences and not stealing because the payers parted with both possession and ownership in the money paid to him.

It has been suggested in a case that the practice known as "money-doubling" constitutes the felony of obtaining by false pretences. This will depend on the facts of each particular case.

If the arrangement is that the money-doubler will return to the client the identical money he received plus some other money, then the offence is stealing because the money-doubler has merely possession of the money. But if ownership of the client's money is intended to pass to the money-doubler the offence is obtaining by false pretences.

In an old case it was held that where a defendant ordered food in a restaurant without making any verbal representation and was found to have no money to pay for the food he ordered, he was not guilty of obtaining the food by false pretences because his conduct did not imply that he was a man of means. But in a later case that view was rejected and it was held that where a new customer ordered a meal in a restaurant, he must be held to make an implied representation that he can and will pay for it before he leaves.

The representation must refer to a matter of fact either past or present. If it relates to future no offence of obtaining by false pretences is committed. When an accused was charged with false pretences the allegation being that he with intent to defraud, obtained a sum of money from another person by falsely pretending that he would give it to a man to give a job to that person, it was held that the accused was not guilty of obtaining money by false pretences because the representation related only to a future matter.

Cheating

Any person who by means of any fraudulent trick or device obtains from any other person anything capable of being stolen or induces any other person to deliver to any person anything capable of being stolen or to pay or deliver to any person any money or goods or any greater sum of money or greater quantity of goods than he would have paid or delivered but for such trick or device is guilty of a misdemeanour, and is liable to imprisonment for two years. A person found committing the offence or cheating may be arrested without warrant.

Conspiracy to Defraud

Any person who conspires with another by deceit or any fraudulent means to affect the market price of anything publicly sold, or to defraud the public, or any person, whether a particular person or not, or to extort any property from any person is guilty of a felony, and is liable to imprisonment for seven years. The offender cannot be arrested without warrant.

Receiving Stolen Property

Any person who received anything which has been obtained by means of any act constituting a felony or misdemeanour, or by means of any act done at a place not in Nigeria which if it had been done in Nigeria would have constituted a felony or misdemeanour, and which is an offence under the laws sin force in the place where it was done, knowing the same to have been so obtained, is guilty of a felony

If the offence by means of which the thing was obtained is a felony, the offender is liable to imprisonment for fourteen years, except in the case in which the thing so obtained was postal matter or any chattel, money or valuable security contained therein, in which case the offender is liable to imprisonment for life. In any other case the offender is liable to imprisonment for seven years.

For the purpose of proving the receiving of anything it is sufficient to show that the accused person has either alone or jointly with some other person had the thing in his possession or has aided in concealing it or disposing of it.

A person charged with receiving must have the thing in his possession, whether alone or jointly with another or has actually aided in concealing or disposing of it.

Possession of a Thing Reasonably Suspected to Have Been Stolen

Every person who is charged before any court with having in his possession or under his control in any manner or in any place, or for that he at any time within the three months immediately preceding the making of the complaint did have in his possession or under his control in any manner or in any place anything which is reasonably suspected of having been stolen or unlawfully obtained and who does not give an account to the satisfaction of the court, as to how he came by the same is guilty of an offence and is liable on conviction, to a fine of two hundred naira or to imprisonment for six months.

Where any person is charged before any court with having or with having had in his possession or under his control in any manner or in place anything which has been stolen or unlawfully obtained or which is reasonably suspected of having been stolen or unlawfully obtained and declares that he received the same for some other person, or that he was employed as a carrier, agent or servant for some other person the court is authorised and required if practicable, to cause every such other person and also if necessary every former or pretended purchaser or other person through whose possession such thing as aforesaid has passed or who has had control thereof to be brought before it and to examine witnesses upon oath touching the same, and if it appears to the court that any person has had possession or control of such thing and had reasonable cause to believe the same to have been stolen or unlawfully obtained every such persons shall be deemed to have had possession or control of such thing at the time and place when and where the same was found or seized and shall be guilty of an offence and liable on conviction to a fine of two hundred naira or to imprisonment for six months.

The possession of or control by a carrier, agent or servant shall be deemed to be the possession of or control by the person who employed such carrier, agent or servant to have or deal with such thing and such person shall be liable, on conviction, to the punishment herein mentioned.

The offender may be arrested without warrant.

CHAPTER 12

Forgery and False Accounting

Forgery

A person who makes a false document or writing knowing it to be false and with intent that it may in any way be used or acted upon as genuine, whether in Nigeria or elsewhere, to the prejudice of any person or with intent that any person may in the belief that it is genuine be induced to do or refrain from doing any act, whether in Nigeria or elsewhere, is said to forge the document or writing.

A person who makes a counterfeit seal or mark or makes an impression of a counterfeit representation of the impression of a genuine seal, with intent in either case that the thing so made may in any way be used or acted upon as genuine, whether in Nigeria or elsewhere, to the prejudice of any person, or with intent that any person may, in the belief that it is genuine, be induced to do or refrain from doing any act, whether in Nigeria or elsewhere, is said to forge the seal or mark.

The term "make a false document or writing" includes altering a genuine document or writing in any material part, either by erasure, obliteration, removal or otherwise, and making any material addition to the body of a genuine document or writing; and adding to a genuine document or writing any false date, attestation, seal or other material matter.

It is immaterial in what language a forged document or writing is expressed. It is immaterial that the forger of anything forged may not have intended that any particular person should use or act upon it, or do or refrain from doing any act.

It is immaterial that the thing forged is incomplete or does not purpose to be a document, writing or seal which would be binding in law for any particular purpose if it is so made and is of such a kind, as to indicate that it was intended to be used or acted upon.

A false document is one which tells a lie about itself. Any addition to the body of a document which is calculated to disarm suspicion is a material addition.

Punishment of Forgery

Any person who forges any document, writing or seal is guilty of an offence which unless otherwise stated is a felony and is liable if no other punishment is provided, to imprisonment for three years.

If the thing forged is a public seal of Nigeria, any State of Nigeria, or of any country in the Commonwealth or is a document affixed to such seal, the offender is liable to imprisonment for life. In other cases of forgeries, the offender is guilty of a felony and is liable to imprisonment for fourteen years.

An untrue statement in a writ that an order of court had been obtained to sell the defendant's immovable property rendered the writ a false document. Altering or adding to the amount on a voucher or cheque makes it a false document. So is signing of a document in the name of another person or a non-existent person.

In a decided case, the appellant endorsed a cheque which was not meant for him in the name of a fictitious person B. E. This was held not to be forgery as the bank officials knew they were dealing with the appellant, even though they did not know his true name.

It is forgery to insert in a document a false date, or place of making where these are material. Where a document purports to bear the thumb print of an illiterate and a false verification of the thumb print, the two are inseparable and the document is a false document.

Uttering False Documents and Counterfeit Seals

Any person who knowingly and fraudulently utters a false document or writing, or a counterfeit seal, is guilty of an offence of the same kind and is liable to the same punishment as if he had forged the thing in question. It is immaterial whether the false document or writing or counterfeit seal, was made in Nigeria or elsewhere.

The term "fraudulently" means an intention that the thing in question shall be used or acted upon as genuine whether in Nigeria or elsewhere, to the prejudice of some person whether a particular person or not or that some person whether a particular person or not or that some persons whether a particular person or not shall in the belief that the thing in question is genuine, be induced to do or refrain from doing some act, whether in Nigeria or elsewhere.

Any person who utters cancelled or exhausted documents or cancelled stamps is guilty of an offence of the same kind and is liable to the same punishment as if he had forged them.

Preparation of Forgery Instruments and Materials for Forgery

Any person who without lawful authority of excuse, the proof of which lies on him –

1. makes or begins or prepares to make, or uses or knowingly has in his possession or disposes of, any paper resembling any paper such as is especially provided by the proper authority for the purpose of being used for making any of the following things:

    (a)   any document acknowledging or being evidence of the indebtedness of the Government of any Commonwealth country; or of any foreign Prince or State, or of any person carrying on the business of banking to any person, or

    (b)   any stamp, licence, permit, or other document, used for the purposes of the public revenue of Nigeria or of any part of Nigeria or of any part of a

Commonwealth country, or any country under the protection of a Commonwealth country, or

(c) any bank note, or any machinery or instrument or material for making such paper or capable of producing in or on paper any words, figures, letters, marks, or lines used in or on paper specially provided for any such purposes, or

2. impresses or makes upon any plate or materials any words, figures, letters, marks, or lines, the print whereof resembles in whole or in part, the words, figures, letters, marks or lines used in any such document as aforesaid; or

3. uses or knowingly has in his possession or disposes of, any plate or material upon which any such words, figures, letters, marks or lines are impressed or made; or

4. uses or knowingly has in his possession or disposes of, any paper on which is written or printed the whole or any part of the usual contents of any such documents as aforesaid;

is guilty of a felony, and is liable to imprisonment for fourteen years, and any such paper, document, bank note, or any machinery or instrument or material for making or capable of producing such paper, document or bank note which are found in his possession shall be forfeited to the State by order of the court before which he is tried or if there is no trial by order of the court before which the offence is inquired into.

Infringing Copyright Works

Any person who knowingly:

(a) makes for sale or hire any infringing copy of a work in which copyright subsists, or

(b) sells or lets for hire or by way of trade exposes or offers for sale or hire any infringing copy of any such work, or

(c) distributes infringing copies of any work for the purposes of trade or to such an extent as to effect prejudicially the owner of the copyright, or

(d) by way of trade exhibits in public any infringing of any such work;

is guilty of a simple offence and is liable to fine not exceeding four hundred naira in respect of the same transaction or in the case of a second or subsequent offence either to such fine or to imprisonment for two months.

Trustees Fraudulently Disposing of Trust Property

Any person who, being a trustee of any property, destroys the property with intent to defraud, or with intent to defraud, converts the property to any use not authorised by the trust, is guilty of a felony and is liable to imprisonment for seven years. The offender cannot be arrested without warrant.

If civil proceedings have been taken against a trustee in respect of any act done by him which is an offence under the provisions of this section, he cannot be afterwards prosecuted for the same cause as for an offence, on the complaint of the person by whom civil proceedings were taken without the sanction of the court or judge before whom the civil proceedings were or are pending.

"Trustees" includes the following persons and no others:

(a) trustees upon express trusts created by a deed, will, or instrument in writing, whether for a public or private or charitable purpose;

(b) trustees appointed by or under the authority of an ordinance, law or statute for any such purpose;

(c) person upon whom the duties of any such trust as aforesaid devolve;

(d) executors and administrators.

Fraudulent False Accounting

Any person who being a clerk or servant, does any of the following acts with intent to defraud, that is:

(a) destroys, alters, mutilates, or falsifies any books, document, valuable security or account which belongs to or is in the possession of his employer or has been received by him on account of his employer, or any entry in such book, document, or account or is privy to any such act, or

(b) makes, or is privy to making any false entry in any such book, document or account; or

(c) omits or is privy to omitting material particular from any such book, document, or account;

is guilty of a felony and is liable to imprisonment for seven years.

To establish a case under this provision the prosecution must not only prove that the accused omitted to make the entry but must also prove that it was his duty to have made it.

Personation Generally

Any person who, with intent to defraud any person, falsely represents himself to be some other person, living, or dead is guilty of a felony and is liable to imprisonment for three years. If the representation is that the offender is a person entitled by will or operation of law to any specific property and he commits the offence to obtain such property or possession thereof, he is liable to imprisonment for fourteen years.

Any person who, without lawful authority or excuse, the proof of which lies on him makes, in the name of any other person before any court or person lawfully authorised to take such an acknowledgement, an acknowledgement of liability of any kind, or an acknowledgement of a deed or other instrument, is guilty of a felony and is liable to imprisonment for seven years.

Personation of a Person Named in a Certificate

Any person who utters any document which has been issued by lawful authority to another person, and whereby that other person is certified to be a person possessed of any qualification recognised by law for any purpose, or to be the holder of any office, or to be entitled to exercise any profession, trade, or business, or to be entitled to any right or privilege, or to enjoy any rank or status, and falsely represents himself to be the person named in the document, is guilty of an offence of the same kind and is liable to the same punishment as if he had forged the document.

CHAPTER 13

Offences Against Liberty

Kidnapping

Any person who:

(a) unlawfully imprisons any person, and takes him out of Nigeria, without his consent; or

(b) unlawfully imprisons any person within Nigeria in such a manner as to prevent him from applying to a court for his release or from discovering to any other person the place where he is imprisoned or in such a manner as to prevent any person entitled to have access to him from discovering the place where he is imprisoned;

is guilty of a felony and is liable to imprisonment for seven years.

Deprivation of Liberty

Any person who unlawfully confines or detains another in any place against his will, or otherwise unlawfully deprives another of his personal liberty, is guilty of a misdemeanour and is liable to imprisonment for two years.

Slave Dealing

Any person who:

(1) deals or trades in, purchases, sells, transfers, or takes any slave;

(2) deals or trades in, purchases, sells, transfers or takes any person in order or so that such person should be held or treated as a slave;

(3) places or receives any person in servitude as a pledge or security for debt whether then due and owing or to be incurred or contingent, whether under the name of a pawn or by whatever other name such person may be called or known;

(4) conveys or induces any person to come within the limits of Nigeria in order or so that such person should be held, possessed, dealt or traded in, purchased, sold or transferred as a slave, or to be placed in servitude as a pledge or security for debt;

(5) conveys or sends or induces any person to go out of the limits of Nigeria in order or so that such person should be possessed, dealt or traded in, purchased, sold or transferred as a slave, or to be placed in servitude as a pledge or security for debt;

(6) whether or not a citizen of Nigeria holds or possesses in Nigeria any person as a slave;

(7) enters into any contract or agreement with or without consideration for doing any of the acts or accomplishing any of the purposes herein above enumerated;

is guilty of slave dealing and is liable for imprisonment for fourteen years.

Treating a person as a slave means treating him as a human chattel and the ultimate use or abuse to which he may be or to be put as chattel is immaterial in deciding whether an offence under slave dealing has been committed.

CHAPTER 14

Miscellaneous Offences

Offences Relating to Currency

Any person who makes or begins to make any counterfeit currency, gold or silver coins is guilty of a felony and is liable to imprisonment for life. Where a person has ten or more unfinished counterfeit coins in his possession the court may presume that he has made them or has been participant in the act of making them unless he proves the contrary.

Preparation for making gold and silver coins is a felony punishable with life imprisonment. Unlawful inquiries with the object of making counterfeit coins constitute an offence and the offender is liable to imprisonment for one year.

A person commits the offence of clipping when he deals with any currency, gold or silver coin in such a manner as to diminish its weight with intent that when so dealt with it may pass as currency, gold or silver coin. The offender is guilty of a felony and is liable to imprisonment for life.

Any person who utters any counterfeit currency, gold or silver coin, knowing it to be counterfeit, is guilty of a misdemeanour and is liable to imprisonment for two years. Any person who commits the offence of uttering after previous conviction is guilty of a felony and is liable to imprisonment for life.

Counterfeiting nickel coins is a felony punishable with seven years imprisonment. Uttering base nickel coins is a misdemeanour and the offender is liable to imprisonment for one year. Defacing coins by stamping words thereon is a misdemeanour punishable with imprisonment for one year.

Offences Relating to Posts and Telecommunications

Any person who stops a mail with intent to search or rob postal matter is guilty of a felony, and is liable to imprisonment for life.

Intercepting telegrams or postal matter is a felony and the offender is liable to imprisonment for life.

Tampering with telegrams or postal matter is a felony punishable with three years imprisonment.

Obtaining telegrams or postal matter by false pretences is a misdemeanour and the offender is liable to imprisonment for two years.

Unlawful hawking of letters is punishable with a fine of two hundred naira.

It is a misdemeanour to send dangerous or obscene things by post. The offender is liable to imprisonment for one year.

Any person who obstructs or delays mails is guilty of a simple offence and is liable to a fine of one hundred naira.

Arson

Any person who wilfully and unlawfully sets fire to any of the following things:

(a) any building or structure whatever, whether completed or not;

(b) any vessel, whether complete or not

(c) any stack of cultivated vegetable produce or of mineral or vegetable fuel;

(d) a mine or the workings, fittings, or appliances of a mine;

is guilty of a felony, and is liable to imprisonment for life.

An attempt to commit arson is a felony punishable with fourteen years imprisonment.

Advertising a Reward for the Return of Stolen or Lost Property

Any person who:

(1) publicly offers a reward for the return of any property which has been stolen or lost, and in the offer makes use of any words purporting that no questions will be asked, or that the person producing such property will not be seized or molested; or

(2) publicly offers to return to any person who may have bought or advanced money by way of loan upon any stolen or lost property the money so paid or advanced, or any other sum of money or reward for the return of such property; or

(3) prints or publishes any such offer;

is guilty of a simple offence and is liable to a fine of one hundred naira.

Offences Relating to Marriage

Bigamy

Any person who having a husband or wife living, marries in any case in which marriage is void by reason of its taking place during the life of such husband or wife, is guilty of a felony, that is bigamy and is liable to imprisonment for seven years. This section does not extend to any person whose marriage with such husband or wife has been dissolved or declared void by a court of competent jurisdiction, nor to any person who contracts a marriage during the life of a former husband or wife, if such husband or wife at the time of the subsequent marriage shall have been absent from such person for the space of seven years, and shall not have been heard of by such person as being alive within that time.

Child Stealing

Any person who, with intent to deprive any parent, guardian, or other person who has the lawful care or charge of a child under the age of twelve years, of the possession of such child, or with intent to steal any article upon or about the person of any such child:

(1) forcibly or fraudulently takes or entices away, or detains the child; or

(2) receives or harbours the child knowing it to have been so taken or enticed away or detained;

is guilty of a felony, and is liable to imprisonment for fourteen years.

It is a defence to a charge of any of the offences defined under this heading to prove that the accused person claimed in good faith a right to the possession of the child, or in the case of an illegitimate child is its mother or claimed to be his father.

CHAPTER 15

Corrupt Practices and Other Related Offences Act, 2000

Sections 1 and 2 of the Corrupt Practices and Other Related Offences Act, 2000 (hereinafter called "The Act") deal with Title, Commencement and Interpretation.

Sections 3 – 6 deliberate on Establishment of Commission, appointment, powers and duties of officers of the Commission.

Section 7 covers standing order while Sections 8 – 26 enumerate the offences and their penalties.

Sections 27 – 42 set out powers of investigation, search, seizure and arrest of the Commission.

Provisions relating to the Chairman of the Commission are mentioned in Sections 43 –.52.while Sections 53 – 66 deal with evidence in the trial of accused persons. The prosecution and trial of offences are highlighted in Sections 61-64.

Sixteen corrupt practices and other related offences are created in Sections 8 –10, 12 – 13, 15 – 19 and 21 – 26 of the Act. Section 11 does not create an offence but states that in the proceedings under the Act, it shall not be necessary that a public officer counselled the commission of an offence. Section 14 also does not create any offence but gives penalty for offences under Section 13. Section 20 gives the penalty for offences under Sections 8 – 19 where penalty is not otherwise stated. The Act is popularly called and known as **anti-corruption law.**

In this book, we are mainly concerned with the treatment of the criminal offences in the Act.

Section 8(1)   stipulates that:

(1) Any person who corruptly –

(a) asks for, receives or obtains any property or benefit of any kind for himself or for any other person; or

(b) agrees or attempts to receive or obtain any property or benefit of any kind for himself or for any person, on account of

    (i)   anything already done or omitted to be done, . . . or

    (ii)   anything to be afterwards done or omitted to be done . . .

is guilty of official corruption and is liable to imprisonment for seven years.

Official corruption is also contained in the Criminal Code. The discussion on this subject in chapter 3 will therefore with some modifications apply to official corruption under the Act. "Public Officer" under the Act include judicial officers serving in Magistrate, Area or Customary Courts or Tribunals.

But under the Criminal Code Act, official corruption cannot be committed by a judicial officer or an officer doing judicial function or any job touching the administration of justice. In the Code, judicial officers may commit the offence of judicial corruption only, not official corruption:

Section 9(1) states:

9(1)   Any person who corruptly –

    (a) gives, confers or procures any property or benefit of any kind to, on or for a public officer or to, on or for any other person; or

    (b) promises or offers to give, confers, procures or attempts to procure any property or benefit of any kind to, on or for a public officer or any other person on account of any such act, omission, favour or disfavour to be done or shown by the public officer; is guilty of an offence of official corruption and shall on conviction be liable to imprisonment for seven years.

Sub-section 9(1)(a) will apply where a person actually gives any property or benefit or benefits for a favour to be done to him. Section 9(1)(b) can be invoked where only an attempt is made to give any property or benefit for a favour or disfavour. Attempt under the Act is wide and an offence may be committed where the defendant only makes preparation to give the property or benefit.

For instance, if a person intends to give money to a public officer, he goes to the bank to withdraw the money or borrows it from a friend. He envelopes the money and writes the name of the public officer on the envelope. He goes to the public officer to give him the envelope containing money but the public officer was not at home. These steps will constitute enough preparation to warrant conviction under Section 9(1)(b) of the Act.

Moreover, official corruption under the Criminal Code Act pertains to corrupt offers made for any benefit or favour shown now or in the past. It does not pertain to favour to be shown in the future, as Section 9(1)(b) of the Act seems to suggest.

Section 10 deals with corrupt demands by any person for anything already done or omitted to be done or any favour or disfavour already shown or anything to be afterwards done or omitted to be done. The offender is guilty of official corruption and is liable to imprisonment for seven years.

Section 10(a)(ii) refers to anything to be afterwards done or omitted, or any favour or disfavour to be afterwards shown to any person, by a public officer in the discharge of his duties. This shows that a favour or disfavour to be shown in the future is caught by the provision.

Section 12 of the Act makes fraudulent acquisition of property an offence and the offender is liable on conviction to imprisonment for seven years. A public officer may be convicted of this offence if he acquired a private interest in any contract, agreement, or investment emanating from or connected with the department or office in which he is employed. But he can acquire interest as a member of a registered joint stock company consisting of more than twenty members.

Section 13 says:

> Any person who receives anything, which has been obtained by means of act constituting a felony or misdemeanour, or by means of any act done at a place outside Nigeria, which if it had been done in Nigeria would have constituted a felony or misdemeanour and which is an offence under the laws in force in the place where it was done, knowing the same to have been so obtained, is guilty of a felony.

According to Section 14 if the offence by means of which the thing was obtained is a felony, the offender shall on conviction be liable to imprisonment for three years. Under Section 20 of the Act the offender shall forfeit the gratification and pay a fine of not less than five times the sum or value of the gratification which is the subject matter of the offence where such gratification is capable of being valued or is of a pecuniary nature, or ten thousand naira, whichever is the higher.

Section 15 of the Act says:

15. Any person who, with intent to defraud or conceal a crime or frustrate the Commission in its investigation of any suspected crime of corruption under the Act or under any other law;

(a) destroys, alters, mutilates, falsifies any book, document, valuable security, account, computer print-out or other electronic device which belongs to or is in the possession of his employer, or has been received by him on account of his employment; or any entry in any such books, document, accounts or electronic device, or is privy to any such act; or

(b) makes or is privy to making any false entry in any such book, document, account or electronic record; or

(c) omits, or is privy to omitting any material particular from such book, document, account or electronic record; is guilty of a felony, and shall on conviction be liable to seven years imprisonment. This offence encompasses destroying evidence, fraudulent false accounting and forgery in the Criminal Code Act.

Section 16 of the Act States:

Any person who, being an officer charged with receipt, custody, use or management of any part of the public revenue or property, knowingly furnishes any false statement or return in respect of any money or property in his possession or under his control;

is guilty of an offence and shall on conviction be liable to seven years imprisonment.

This offence is similar to false statements by officials of companies under the Code. A document may be false in a material particular although no one specific statement in it can be proved to be false if, taken as a whole, what it implies is false on account of what it does not state. Alteration in or addition to a document makes it false. So is signing of a document in the name of another person or of a non-existent person.

Section 17 (1) states:

Any person who corruptly:

(a) accepts, obtains or agrees to accept or attempts to obtain from any person for himself or for any other person any gift or consideration as an inducement or reward for doing or forebearing to do any act or thing;

(b) gives or agrees to give or offers any gift or consideration to any agent as an inducement or reward for doing or forebearing to do any act, or thing or;

(c) knowingly gives to any agent, or being an agent knowingly uses with intent to deceive the principal . . . and which to his knowledge, is intended to mislead his principal or any other person;

is guilty of an offence and shall on conviction be liable to five years imprisonment.

This offence is known as gratification by and through agents. If a principal asks an agent to take a bribe for and on his behalf, the principal cannot escape liability merely because he did not receive the bribe with his own hands. Except the agent is acting under compulsion both the principal and the agent are liable. The act of the agent is that of the principal.

"Consideration" in this section includes valuable consideration of any kind. The expression, "agent" includes any person employed by or acting for another; while "principal" includes an employer.

Section 18 of the Act stipulates

Any person who offers to any public officer, or being a public officer solicits, counsels, or accepts any gratification as an inducement or a reward for:

(a) voting or abstaining from voting at any meeting of the public body in favour or against any measure, resolution or question submitted to the public body;

(b) performing or abstaining from performing or aiding in procuring, expediting, delaying, hindering or preventing the performance of any official act;

(c) aiding in procuring or preventing the passing of any vote or the granting of any contract, award, recognition or advantage in favour of any person; or

(d) showing or forebrearing to show any favour or disfavour in his capacity as such officer, shall notwithstanding that the officer did not have the power, right or opportunity so to do, or that the inducement or reward was not in relation to the affairs of the public body;

be guilty of an offence and shall on conviction be liable to five years imprisonment with hard labour.

The above is the offence of bribery concerning public officers. Both the person who offers the gratification and the person who accepts it are guilty of this offence. The gratification may be given to a public officer to induce him to vote one way or the other for a measure or resolution submitted to the public body. It may also be given to delay, hinder or prevent the performance of an official act or to aid in procuring or preventing the grant of any contract or award. It is no defence that the public officer has no power, right or opportunity to grant or prevent the grant of any favour or reward.

Section 19 of the Act deals with a public officer using his office or position for gratification. The offender shall on conviction be liable to imprisonment for five years without option of fine. Any public officer who uses his office or position to gratify or confer any corrupt or unfair advantage upon himself or any relation or associate of the public officer or any other public officer is guilty of this offence.

In my view, any public officer who uses his position corruptly or unfairly to get a job for his relation or any other person will be guilty of an offence under this section. So will a public officer who uses his position corruptly or unfairly to secure admission for his son or daughter in a school or any institution of learning. The facts of each case would determine whether the public officer used his position to gain a corrupt or unfair advantage.

Section 21 of the Act states:

21(1)   Any person who, without lawful authority or reasonable excuse, offers any advantage to any other person as an inducement to or reward for or otherwise on account of that other person refraining or having refrained from bidding at any auction conducted by or on behalf of any public body, shall be guilty of an offence.

(2)   Any person who, without lawful authority or reasonable excuse, solicits or accepts any advantage as an inducement to or reward for or otherwise on account of

his refraining or having refrained from bidding at **any** auction conducted by or on behalf of any public body, shall be guilty of an offence.

This offence may be committed by a person who has inside knowledge of the property to be auctioned. There may be some defects on the property to be auctioned, which defects are unknown to the auctioneers or bidders. If a person who knows of these defects tells the prospective bidder of the defects for a reward and the latter refrains from bidding at the auction, that person will be guilty of an offence under this provision.

Under Sub-section (3) of Section 21 of the Act, any person guilty of an offence under this section shall on conviction on indictment be liable to a fine of the current price of the property and imprisonment for 3 years. The fine at the current price of the property and the imposition of three years are cumulative.

Section 22(1) states:

Any person who, without lawful authority or reasonable excuse, offers an advantage to a public servant as an inducement to or reward for or otherwise on account of such public servant's giving assistance or using influence in, or having given assistance or used influence in:

(a) the promotion, executing, or procuring of –

(i) any contract . . . or

(ii) sub-contract . . . or

(b) payment of the price in any such contract or sub-contract shall be guilty of an offence.

(2) Any public servant who, without lawful authority or reasonable excuse, solicits or accepts any advantage as an inducement to or reward for or otherwise on account of his giving assistance or using influence in, or having given assistance or used influence in:

(a) the promotion, execution or procuring, or

(b) the payment of the price, consideration, or

(c) other moneys stipulated or otherwise provided for in, any contact or sub-contact as is referred to in sub-section 1 shall be guilty of an offence.

Any person or public officer who commits an offence under Sub-sections (1) and (2) shall be liable on conviction to a term of imprisonment for seven years or a one million naira fine.

Sub-section (3) of Section 22 renders any public officer who in the course of his official duties, inflates the price of any goods or services above the prevailing market price or professional standard guilty of an offence punishable with seven years imprisonment and a fine of one million naira. If a department of Government is selling fertiliser at a fixed market price, a public officer who sells above the market price will be guilty of an offence under this sub-section. The punishment is rather severe.

The offences in Sub-sections 4 and 5 of Section 22 have hitherto been administrative or financial directives conveyed to public officers in Circulars and Financial Instructions. They are now made law. It is therefore an offence to award or sign any contract without budget provision, approval and cash backing. The offender on conviction is liable to three years imprisonment and a fine of one hundred thousand naira. It is also an offence for any public officer to transfer or spend money allocated for a particular project or service to another project or service. A public officer convicted of this offence is liable to one year imprisonment or a fine of fifty thousand naira.

Under Section 23 (1) of the Act, it is the duty of any public officer to report bribery transactions to the nearest officer of the Commission or police officer. He should also give the name if known of the person who gave, promised or offered the gratification. Under Section 23(2), any soliciting or obtaining or attempt to obtain gratification must also be reported to the nearest officer of the Commission or police officer with the name if known or full description of the person who solicited or attempted to obtain the gratification. Under Sub-sections (3) any person who fails, without reasonable excuse, to comply with sub-sections (1) and (2) shall be guilty of an offence and shall on conviction be liable to a fine not exceeding one hundred thousand naira or to imprisonment for a term not exceeding two years or to both fine and imprisonment.

Section 24 of the Act makes any dealing with property acquired through gratification an offence punishable with a term of imprisonment not exceeding five years. This offence is committed by any person who, whether within or outside Nigeria directly or indirectly enters into any dealing in relation to any property or any part thereof which was the subject matter of an offence under Sections 10, 11, 12 and 13-20. It is submitted that before a person can be convicted of this offence he must know or must have with reasonable diligence known that the property was acquired through gratification.

Section 25 makes it an offence to make false or mis-leading statements.

Subsection (1) stipulates that –

Any person who makes or causes any other person to make to an officer of the Commission or to any other Public Officer, in the course of the exercise by such Public Officer of the duties of his office, any statement which to the knowledge of the person making the statement or causing the statement to be made –

(a) is false, or intended to mislead or is untrue in any material particular; or

(b) is not consistent with any other statement previously made by such person . . .;
shall be guilty of an offence and shall on conviction be liable to a fine not exceeding One hundred thousand naira or to imprisonment for a term not exceeding two years or to both such fine and imprisonment.

It is also an offence to make a statement to an officer of the Commission or to the Attorney-General and subsequently make an inconsistent statement to an officer of the Commission or such other public officer. The offender shall on conviction be liable to a fine not exceeding ten thousand naira or to imprisonment for a term not exceeding two years or to both. The prosecutor must prove that the defendant knew that the statement he made was false or misleading.

It must be noted that for the purpose of sub-sections (1) and (2), any statement made in the course of any legal proceedings before the court, whether civil or criminal, or any statement made by any person in the course of any disciplinary proceedings, whether such legal proceedings or disciplinary proceedings are against the person making the statement or against any other person, shall be deemed to be a statement made to a person having authority or power under the law to receive the statement so made.

Section 26 (1) states:
Any person who –

   (a) attempts to commit any offence under this Act;

   (b) does any act preparatory to or in furtherance of the commission of any offence under this Act; or

   (c) abets or is engaged in a criminal conspiracy to commit any offence under this Act;

   (d) commits any offence under this Act;

   shall be guilty of an offence and shall, on conviction, be liable to the punishment provided for such offence.

(2) Prosecution for an offence under this Act shall be initiated by the Attorney-General of the Federation, or any person or authority to whom he shall delegate his authority, in any superior court of record so designated by the Chief Judge of a State or the Chief Judge of the Federal Capital Territory, Abuja.

(3) Prosecution for an offence shall be concluded and judgment delivered within ninety working days of its commencement save that the jurisdiction of the court to continue to hear and determine the case shall not be affected where good grounds exist for a delay.

Attempt under this provision is wider than attempt in the Code or under the Common Law. Section 26 (1) (b) makes any act preparatory to or in furtherance of the commission of any offence punishable like an attempt. In an English case, the accused entered for an athletics meeting and filled in the entry form falsely that he had never won a race. He thus obtained a favourable handicap and won the races. He never had a chance to apply for the prizes before his arrest. He was found guilty of an attempt to obtain by false pretences. At the stage he filled the entry form, he was guilty of an act preparatory to or in furtherance of the commission of an offence under Section 26 (1) (b) of the Act.

In another case, a jeweller hid his jewellery, tied himself up and pretended that his shop was burgled. He did this so that he might get money from his insurance company for the loss of his jewellery. He was arrested before he made any claim. It was held that his action had not reached the stage of attempt. Under Section 26 (1) (b) of the Act he will be guilty of doing an act preparatory to or in furtherance of the commission of the offence in question. Mere preparation and attempt carry the same punishment. Thus under the Act, mere preparation to offer or accept a bribe is punishable under section 26 (1) (b).

Section 26 (1) (c) deals with criminal conspiracy, and what obtained under conspiracy in chapter 2 of this book will apply to this subsection of the Act. Abetting conspirators is an offence under the Act.

Index

Penal servitude, 37
Penalty, 74
Perjury, 29-30
Personal liberty
— deprivation of, 68
Personation
— of a person named in Certif-
icate, 66-67
Personation Generally, 66
Possession of Stolen Property, 59-60
Principal offenders, 2-3, 9
Procuration, 34
Prostitution, 36-37
— persons trading in, 34-35
Provocation, 40, 46-47
Public law
— breach of, 1
Public
— Officer, 75-76, 79-80, 83
— Order Decree, 22
— Servant, 81

Rape, 41-42
Receiving Stolen Property, 58
Reward
— for return of stolen or lost
property, 72
Riot, 22, 45
Riotous assembly, 22
Robbery, 53-54
— and firearms (Special
Provisions)
Decree, 53
Rogues and Vagabonds, 36-37

Secret
— cults, 21
— societies, 21

Sedition, 17-19
Seditious intention, 18
Self
— control
— loss of, 46
— defence, 45
— aiding in, 45
Simple offences, 1
Slave Dealing, 68-69
Society, 20-21
Stealing, 48-53
— punishment of, 50-52
Suppression of riot, 45

Testamentary instrument, 50-52
Testimony, 29
Tort, 1
Treason
— concealment of, 16
— punishment for, 15
Treasonable felonies, 16
Trust Property
— fraudulent disposal of, 65
Trustees, 65

Unlawful
— Assemblies, 21-23
— Carnal knowledge, 33
— Societies, 20-21
— Society
— management of, 21
Unnatural offences, 33-35

Violation of the laws, 21
Violence, 18-19

Witchcraft, 6-7

www.ingramcontent.com/pod-product-compliance
Lightning Source LLC
Chambersburg PA
CBHW061835220326
41599CB00027B/5293